THE GO
CELLAR G

CW00725053

THE GOOD CELLAR GUIDE

HOW TO BUY AND STORE WINE FOR PLEASURE AND PROFIT

Jón Thorn

SIDGWICK & JACKSON
LONDON

To my mother and father

First published in Great Britain in 1990
by Sidgwick & Jackson Limited

Copyright © 1990 by Jón Thorn
Illustrations © by Celia Lyttelton 1990

ISBN 0-283-99952-7

Typeset by Rowland Phototypesetting Limited
Bury St Edmunds, Suffolk

Printed in Great Britain by
Mackays of Chatham plc, Chatham, Kent

for Sidgwick & Jackson Limited
1 Tavistock Chambers, Bloomsbury Way
London WC1A 2SG

Contents

Acknowledgments

This book could not have been started or finished without the kindness and help of a number of people and organizations: Queen Mary College, London School of Economics, David Litchfield, *A la Carte*, Vicky Jones, Glynn Christian, Carolyn Cavele, Dr John Morrall, Food and Wine from France, Wines from Spain, Portuguese Government Trade Office, Southwark Council, BLPES, Citalia, British Rail and Panasonic.

Special and specific thanks to Bill Hamilton, Oliver Johnson, Hilary Davies, Andrew Armstrong, Lucy Riall, John Wilson, Elena dell'Agnese, Guilio Franzinetti, and Beverly Brittan. A second dedication is due to the late Jeremy Round, a great loss and a great help to me. Thanks also to the tasting team, some of whom want to remain anonymous, and others of whom might be embarrassed if called upon to review a book they contributed to – and I wouldn't want them to feel hidebound in that way.

The longest thanks of all go to my parents, who were there when I needed them, at the very beginning and ever since.

Jón Thorn.

About this Book

The Good Cellar Guide is intended to become an annual wine publication. There are many such books nowadays, but this one has a specific difference: it concerns itself only with wines to buy and keep until mature, not with wines to buy and drink now.

It is intended to save you money, increase your drinking pleasure, expand your wine knowledge, perhaps improve the value of your home, and give advice about wine investment.

The Good Cellar Guide also offers more to read than a series of fifty-word entries with a complicated key to them (although it has these as well). There is a review of wine regions of the world, a full account of the DIY of wine storage, and specific recommendations for over 200 wines to buy and keep, forming a complete reference book for anyone interested in cellaring wine.

Future *Guides* will contain suggestions for many more wines for laying down, from an increased number of retailers, and, in time, perhaps newsletters and offers.

The aim is to get better value for your money by keeping wine. The *Guide* will show you the wines to keep and how to keep them. Once you start down this path, it is a very pleasant and potentially all-consuming one to follow. So let's not drink more, but do let's drink better.

Some notes about some wine words:
Bin An open storage unit where bottles are stored loose.
Classed growth Bordeaux vineyards that were classified in 1855 or later.
Drinking (As in, 'drinking now') – used to describe a wine that is mature.
En primeur Wines that are sold in the cask in Bordeaux; VAT, shipping and duty are added to their price. This is usually the cheapest way to buy quality Bordeaux.
First growths The best wines classified in 1855: Châteaux Latour, Lafite-Rothschild, Margaux, Haut-Brion, Mouton-Rothschild (since 1973).
MW Master of Wine, the top wine qualification.

*'The very best of vineyards
is the cellar.'*
Byron, *Don Juan*, Canto XIII, 76.

1

WHY STORE WINE?

Wine is a pleasure, and an expense. We all buy what we like and what we can afford, and happily, these are exciting times for the wine drinker in the UK. There are more of us, we are spending more per bottle, and we are becoming more knowledgeable about the range of flavours available to us.

The past five to ten years have seen a revolution in wine-production and wine sales. We drink many more wines, from many more parts of the world, made in new, high-tech ways. Most wine is made to be drunk as young as possible, with its fruit intact. These short shelf-life bottles are OK to quaff as part of a meal, but they are only the tip of the iceberg of wine pleasure.

Other wines which can mature over years, even decades, are mostly being drunk far too young. This is a tragic waste. If kept under the right conditions, those bottles could, in a few years, contain a very much better wine, with a richer range of flavours – the sum of all the potential pleasure put into the bottle in the first place. It will also be much better value for money, of course. This book is about how to break the vicious cycle of immaturity, by showing the wine lover how to drink better wine for less money.

Now for the serious bit. This book is also about the practicalities and the pleasures of keeping wine, written for the modern wine drinker, who knows what he or she likes, and wants to find out more. It is independent and has no interest in doing favours for retailers. Wine writing must be about giving consumers the information to find their way through the forests of verbiage and hype all salesmen use. On the whole, the wine trade is staffed by vaguely sympatico types, whose motivations are different from those of double-glazing salesmen. But there is always the bottom line, and that involves getting you to buy their stuff.

So, yes, the consumer is king (end of the serious bit).

New wine regions are becoming popular all the time; Australia today, Chile tomorrow, and all the while France keeps sending us huge amounts of wine. In the US they used to ask 'domestic or imported?' if you asked for wine. Only the most stiffly patriotic Brit would ask the same question. We can pick and choose what we can afford from all over the world. We are also the purest form of wine market an economist could devise, because, of all the wine-drinking countries of the world, historically we have produced the least amount of it ourselves, per capita.

The market for wine in Britain has changed. The days when the people who bought wine would wander in from their club or City institution to choose a few dozen bottles from the only shop they ever bought from are long, long gone. It was the supermarkets, and especially Sainsbury's, who significantly changed how we think about wine. Their huge economies of scale meant they could sell decent wine at a price that was within the pockets of their customers. Alongside this change in supply was a change in demand: more people wanted to drink wine with their food.

Buying wine is no longer an exclusively male task. Once wine stood on shelves beside the rest of the week's shopping, it was the people who usually do that shopping who became the largest buyers of wine in Britain: women.

There is a price to pay for some of these advances. The willingness and ability of wine retailers to store and mature wine over long periods has never been lower; in fact it is non-existent. In the old days (apparently) people either bought barrels of wine and bottled and kept it themselves, or bought from wine merchants fully mature wine which had lain quietly for as many years as it needed.

But today the winemakers all want to sell their bottles as soon as possible, the shippers and middlemen want to unload it as fast as they can, and the retailer wants it to fly out of the door. The result of this drive for profit, by reducing the overhead costs of storage, is that we have never bought and drunk more immature wine than we do today.

We cannot change how the world works but we can break the chain by buying and keeping that wine, at home or somewhere else, and by drinking it when it is mature.

So, why store wine? The main reason is pleasure. It's fun to potter round a cellar you have built or adapted and filled with bottles over the years. The pleasure of owning some good or unusual bottles is a very intense one. There is the anticipation of eventually opening them and choosing which of your friends and relations is worth sharing such vinous enjoyment with.

Certain wines go better with certain foods, and being able to match impulse food purchases makes for a happier meal. There will be moments in your life when the only wine to really hit the spot will be an Oz Chardonnay, or a Chianti Classico, so if you've got some already in stock, it can.

Alternatively, dash out to the off-licence, dash back with a decent bottle, shaking it up all the way, open it and drink immediately. It has already spent two months standing in the bright lights of a warm shop and it doesn't need much imagination to realize that you will not be enjoying this bottle at its best, nor getting good value for money. It pays you to have at least a few bottles of what you fancy at home, getting ready for their big moment in your life.

All of these pleasures combine in a unique way in drinking wine. You choose what you want to drink from among a huge range of possibilities, and you choose how, when and with whom to drink them. No other pleasure we can experience is so complete, or so singularly internal and social at the same time. Food is equally tantalizing and internal but is short-lived, and sex is equally involving, but wine is the only complete sensual and intellectual experience available. Or that's what I reckon.

Reasons for storing wine:
- It is very expensive to buy mature wine.
- The only mature wine available is fine wine – i.e. those wines which are worth someone keeping to sell later at a huge premium.
- Fine wines *are* expensive to buy, even *en primeur*, but if you do buy them you should be able to sell a portion off later to allow you to drink the rest free.
- Although many lower quality wines will keep, there is simply no later opportunity to buy those wines when mature, unless you pay well over the odds for them in a restaurant.
- Once you start buying for more than immediate consumption, you can start to take advantage of your own flexibilities of scale, because you only buy what you want, not what you need to drink. You can combine with friends, form clubs, buy during sales or at auctions; you can buy cheap.
- Because you spent the money years ago, at the time of drinking there is often the pleasing psychological effect that the bottle seems to be 'free'. It's not, of course, but it seems that way.

Above all else, by keeping wine, you will become an intelligent consumer, able to manage the wine market for your convenience and needs. You are getting more value out of your bottles than was in them when they were sold to you. This is the only way to stop being short-changed by the wine market as it exists today, and will probably continue for some time.

A good wine retailer will agree, if pressed, that many of the better wines in the shop are immature by any definition, and he probably wouldn't drink some of them himself. As Good Cellar persons, that suits us just fine, we don't want to pay up to 30 per cent more per bottle for it to be matured by someone else. But there are other retailers, either knaves or fools, who will tell you that this or that bottle is perfectly mature, or they wouldn't be selling it, would they? By claiming that their, say, two-year-old Chablis is ready to drink now, they are either lying to you, and know that they are, or they don't know the difference between mature and immature wine. Go somewhere else.

John Armit.

The future

For a look at what the wine business used to be like, and for a view of what it may become, I talked to John Armit, once a Director of Corney & Barrow, the City firm, who now sells wine on his own account, and he was once described as 'the most dynamic force in the wine business'. He was one of the first British wine merchants actually to wander round vineyards in France looking for exciting wines, and one of the first to get the *en primeur* market off the ground. Sitting now in a cool, high-tech office in Notting Hill he recalled his start in the trade. 'When I arrived at Corney & Barrow there were old men sitting on high stools at Victorian desks filling in large leather-bound books with figures they didn't understand. Corney & Barrow then held huge stocks of mature wine which they were selling by the bottle.

Selling mature wine is certainly one difference between then and now. Another, of course, is that almost no genuine Burgundy reached these shores until after 1971. It was all blended with Rhône wines, or worse, to beef it up.

'Up to the '60s people only bought mature wine, but it was obvious and logical that the burden of storing these wines over a long period should at least in part be met by the customer.' Sadly, of course, it is now being met in full. John himself is coming round more and more to the French way in these things, which is to drink wine much younger than would be considered correct in the UK. 'I've found I like the tannin, and the "grip" of younger wines. In France, they say that as you get older you prefer your wine more mature, and your girls younger. Well, I'm going the other way, as it were, I'm drinking '82s, now, and '81s. Château Cheval Blanc '82 is delicious now.'

A trend that has carried with it both good and bad is the great progress in wine-making technology. It is now possible to make the technically perfect wine, but it also has an international blandness about it. John thinks that the very greatest wines he has tasted have all had some interesting flaw which has enhanced their greatness. He is more hopeful about some of the younger generation of wine-makers who are not infatuated by high-tech catalogues. 'They're making wine more in the style of their grandfathers. It's their fathers who've fouled it up.'

Burgundy means different things to different people, but to almost all of them one thing stands out: it's expensive. John has no sympathy with this view, and talking about it makes him so agitated he has to get up and walk around the room. 'You know, that really gets me. All these people going on about how their families used to be able to afford classed growth Bordeaux and domaine Burgundy, and now they can't.

'The reason for that is the same as with anything of terrific quality and limited supply. In the end, it goes to those who've got it – i.e. money. Since we haven't been competing too well in the world over the last forty years, we can afford to buy less of it than we used to. Now a lot of it goes to the US, Germany, and now Japan.'

Japan's emergence as a wine-drinking nation is a source of bemusement in many parts of the wine world at the moment. John sees Japanese buyers now having the same kind of impact on the market and prices as the entry of the Americans had in the late '60s.

In terms of sources of wine, he is very hopeful about the state of Oregon. 'It's wonderful there. Many of these wine-makers went there in the '60s in the station wagon with *The Whole Earth Catalogue*.

Things are very much better in California also; they're getting away from making "centrefold" style wines, very upfront, and making more complex wines instead. Chilean wines are not bad, but they remind me of how Spanish wine used to taste; how Rioja used to but doesn't anymore. I hope they don't make the same mistake of putting prices up and letting the quality go down. Spain has some great wine-makers, but there is also much that is terrible; it is like how Italy was ten years ago.

'A lot of those wines are "hangover wines". You know, in the first mouthful, "yes, this is going to give me a hangover". I don't know why you know, but you do.'

2

HOW TO STORE WINE

The basics: bottles of wine do best in a constant, cool temperature; they don't like light, and they don't like being shaken about.

Wine is grape juice which has had its chemical character changed by the process of fermentation. This is caused by the action of yeasts present in the atmosphere, and on the grapes, coming into contact with the sugars in the flesh of the grapes, and turning them into alcohol. The process starts when the grapes are crushed, and you can watch it happen in your home. Buy some grapes and some yeast, and mash them up in a bucket which shouldn't be too cold. When a foam spreads across the top of the muck, it has begun fermenting, but it will oxidize unless you put it in something airtight. If you prepare a galvanized dustbin, you could make some wine, after a fashion. Bottle and test some of your friendships by market-researching it. It should be harmless.

The things which make a wine worth drinking

The first of many factors which make a wine worth drinking and, especially, keeping is crop yield. In general, the fewer the grapes produced from any one vine, the better the quality. Many of the appellation controls in Europe are designed to limit the grape yields from vines, and thus act as a basic defence of quality.

We live in very high-tech times as far as wine-making goes. Unbelievable variations and opportunities exist for wine-makers to achieve their aims. This starts with the vine; the basic varieties of vine which are now grown all over the world, such as the Cabernet Sauvignon, or the Chardonnay, are usually grafted onto root stock, to avoid attack by the phylloxera beetle which devastated the French vineyards in the 1870s and 1880s and reached the other European vineyards around the turn of this century.

Technology can add to or diminish a wine's character, but that

15

character is the product of soil, site, and microclimate. Good Champagne needs a chalky soil, while the best parts of the Médoc in Bordeaux lie over gravel. Few areas producing fine wines grow vines on valley floors; vines do better on the less fertile soil of slopes, especially those which get a lot of sun, and where drainage is better. California is famously different, and places such as the Napa Valley are covered, floor and slope, with vines. The New World also believes in irrigating vines, which many appellation areas in Europe forbid, although it certainly does happen, and I saw it happening in the south of France during the hot dry summer of 1989.

After the basics of vine growth come the variations of vine training. Various styles, high, low, bush-like, hanging off wires, spread out or spread over to hide the grapes from the sun under the foliage, are used according to the needs of the area. Vines and their grapes also form tasty or interesting snacks for various mites, bugs and diseases. This is the point at which the Greens start to get worried. Sadly, much of the wine we drink contains a lot of chemicals, or their detritus. Various chemicals are used on the vines and grapes, and some are added to the wine as well. Sulphur dioxide, SO_2, is the wine-maker's magic wand, and with it all manner of problems can be solved. But it also causes a lot of headaches as well, and asthmatics especially should beware of wines with SO_2 in them. Organic wines do exist, but many of them are only half organic; it is a lot easier to grow grapes organically, than it is to vinify them into wine. Once inside the fermenting house, all manner of chemical aids are used. The consolation in drinking quality wines is that there will generally be fewer chemicals in these wines than in really cheap ones, because more effort has gone into making them.

All that skill, effort, craft and knowledge deserves a better fate than to be wasted by being handled wrongly and drunk too early.

Not many people buy their wine in wooden casks these days, although I used to know people who bought their Chianti from the vineyard by the 10-litre or larger glass container, complete with an olive oil slick on top to prevent oxidation. The Tuscan way is to scoop off the oil carefully prior to drinking, or to soak it up on bread, but the impatient thirst of British art students didn't always allow for such niceties.

The normal method of buying wine these days is by the bottle and multiples thereof. There are good commercial reasons why this is the case, but the real and wonderful reason is that wine can improve in the bottle to an otherwise unattainable level.

The strange thing is that we don't really understand how this happens. What we do know is the empirical result of tasting bottles during their cycle of development, and coming to understand how the different changes relate to each other. This is not really a science, yet.

One of the most basic things we don't know is whether there really is a transfer of air through the cork, and if there is, whether this is a good or bad thing. If there is a transfer, and most of the trade believe there is, the amount is too small to be measured. Certainly, over the years a wine shrinks in the bottle, so part of it may have left the bottle, but it may also be the result of chemical action.

At the major industry bash, Vinexpo, in Bordeaux in 1989, the temperature inside the building became so high that corks were being forced out of bottles because the heat was making the wine and air inside them expand. If you've got a bottle with the cork 'peeping' over the lip of the bottle, it may have suffered a similar fate, and won't be at its best. Freezing is less harmful than overheating.

The sediment in the bottle is not a bad thing; it's actually a good thing, because it means that the bottle has aged, and that the wine was not heavily filtered before bottling, which can reduce the character of a wine. The first time I came across a cork with sugar-like tartaric crystals on the wine side, I assumed that someone was trying to poison me with glass; what it means is that at some point the wine has been quite cold, down to 40°F, and these crystals were precipitated.

Three components in wine affect its ageing in the bottle: tannin (in red wine), acidity and fruit. Alcohol is also important, and seems to help preserve the character of the fruit, and to stabilize the chemical composition of the wine.

With young clarets, the annual game with each vintage is to ask yourself how long the tannin will take to mature and fall away to reveal the fruit behind it? That's how a wine's expected maturity curve is judged. The object is to find the 'centre'. This is the perceived point where the potential balance of fruit, tannin and acidity will be revealed. This is done in the first instance by examining the character of the fruit: does it have a 'tight kernel'; is it 'thin', 'loose', 'blowsy', or 'stewed'? Any of these are less desirable, but do not mean that a wine will not come right. Rhône wines have a greater tendency when young to appear stewed, German wines can appear to be thin, Iberian wines are either huge and unapproachable or blowsy.

Wines can 'hibernate' also, by appearing to be 'closed' and 'dumb'. Different wines hibernate at different times, and a whole vintage can go into hibernation and come out around the same time. The Nebbiolo grape used to make Barolo has a great tendency to hibernate over long periods. During hibernation the parameter elements (tannin, acidity and fruit) are noticeable, but the whole feel of the wine is short, and offers no obviously pleasant sensation.

1975 clarets are closed at the moment, and have been so for some time. Some people don't believe they will ever 'come around', because the tannin is still so dense even though some of these wines are turning brown which is a sign that they are approaching full maturity. Other people believe the first growths will come back, but that may be because they paid a lot for them.

In white wine it is the acidity that matures wine; it's that tang that is so noticeable in Sancerre, and is picked up by the sides and the under-neath of the tongue, and by the teeth. In red wines it is the tannin that matures it. Pips, skin and stalks give red wine their tannin. This tastes dry, stalky and harsh and is noticeable at the back of the mouth. What both acid and tannin do is to preserve and mature the fruit, and guide it towards the promised land of mature balance and optimum drinka-bility. The more tannin a red wine has, or acidity a white wine has, the longer it will live, but also the more inaccessible it will be at first. Acidity does exist in red wines, and can also help to age them. The Syrah or Shiraz grape variety can produce a quite acidic red wine, which does not always display tannin very clearly.

Fruit on its own cannot live very long. Beaujolais Nouveau or *primeur* is a perfect example of a red wine with no tannin, since it is fermented with as little contact as possible with the skin, just enough to give it a bit of colour. After six months to a year, the fruit begins to fade, and the wine will taste tired.

The smaller the bottle, the quicker the wine will age. This is partly due to the proportion of the wine in contact with the air in the bottle, and also because the greater volume in the bottle increases the maturation required. Magnums, 1.5 litre-size bottles, are considered the ideal size for Bordeaux to mature in, and one magnum will always cost more than two 75cl bottles.

Ageing: what is it?

There are two kinds of ageing, one is 'oxidative' where the wine is aged in contact with the air in a wooden cask; and the other is 'reductive' where there is no changing air contact in the bottle. Ideally, for quality wines, one to three years' barrel-ageing is used before bottling, and for some even longer. Some wines, like Cham-pagne and vintage Port, mature and develop almost exclusively in the bottle, while others, such as Sherry, are barrel-aged.

We have lived through the barrel wars of late; barrels can be made from new or old oak, from Nevers, Limousin, America, the Baltic or the Balkans, then they can be dried, toasted or steamed, split or sawn, by machine or by hand, and can be made in different sizes. The variations are enormous, and the arguments have raged, mainly in the US, where some of the most arcane tasting sessions have tried to decide between the effects on the wine of the various options. The traditional Bordeaux *barrique* is hand-made from new, untoasted Limousin oak. Other wine-makers use the cheaper method of adding oak chips to the fermenting wine. The taste of oak is desirable because it is seen as adding 'complexity' to wine, but an over-long ageing in the barrel can dry a wine out.

Barrel-ageing has the effect of bringing out certain flavour elements in a wine by a slow aeration, which also protects the wine from some of the effects of oxidation. Tannins are also leached out of the wood into the wine. These, along with infinitesimal oxygenation produce a wine that has a complex chemical structure and it is this increased complexity that adds quality to the finished product.

How long different wines take to get to maturity depends on a number of factors; for example whether they are made from a blend of grape varieties, or of different vintages, and of wines from different sites. The greater the blend, the sooner it will mature. The other factors are the grape variety and how the wine has been made, or vinified. Cabernet Sauvignon, the best known grape of Bordeaux, and the Nebbiolo of Barolo are not varieties that show their charms early, while the Merlot or the Gewürztraminer are much more accessible. The longer a red wine rests on its skins, pips, and stalks the more tannin it will gain, and the longer a white wine rests on its 'lees' (grape debris and dead yeast cells), the longer-lived the wine will be. Beyond these factors, the ripeness of the grapes, and the general conditions of the vintage will all affect the wine.

Bottle care

Once you've got them home, and have made the commitment to keep them until mature, the care of your bottles under the best conditions is important. The five basic needs of wine bottles to mature to good effect are: • dark • still • cool • flat • dry or moist

Of all these, the least observed is **dark**. General light will oxidize wine after some time; that's why the bottle is dark green or brown. Direct sunlight will kill a wine dead in no time at all. Sparkling wines are especially susceptible. One large producer of *sekt* (German sparkling wine) started to sell their wine in clear bottles, as a marketing ploy to make them look different from the rest. I would only have bought it with a guarantee that the particular bottle had been chipped from a tar coffin the day before.

Dry or moist sounds like a contradiction in terms, but ideally we want

19

a bit of both. The atmosphere should be moist enough to keep the corks from drying out, but dry enough to prevent moulds and fungus developing. Whether the temperature is 50°F, 55°F, or 60°F, is not fantastically important, so long as it is more or less constant. Great swings in temperature will tire a wine out, and although warmer conditions will mature a wine more quickly but less fully, this tendency should not be taken to extremes.

In America the idea of temperature-diverse cellars has caught on, where the long-term wines are kept at 50°F, the medium-terms at 55°F, and the drinking wines at 60°F.

All bottles should be stored on their side so that the wine stays in contact with the cork to keep it moist enough to remain airtight. The difference this contact makes can be seen by looking at the difference in size between the wine end and the air end of some corks. The exceptions are most of the fortified wines, such as non-vintage Port, Madeira, and Sherry. One of the worst things seen by a Christie's wine estimator was some '82 Mouton-Rothschild in its wooden box, stored on its end because it could be tucked away conveniently in a space under the stairs. Convenient, but death to the wine in those six bottles no longer in contact with the corks.

Being made of glass, the bottle offers almost perfect conditions for the wine to mature in. The only weak point is the cork; the most important part of bottle care is to look after the cork and capsule.

Good hygiene and tidy habits wherever wine is stored are important, so don't leave rubbish lying around which could generate smells and moulds. Cobwebbed bottles only look good. Hugh Johnson's method of label preservation is to spray it with an odourless hair lacquer (no CFCs please).

Ideally, once a wine has been bottled it should not be moved at all. The reality is that the wine on the supermarket shelf is in trauma; its development has been suspended or even damaged as it struggles under the tripartite attack of recent movement, bright shop lights, and at least two large swings of temperature a day, as the shop heating goes on and off.

The taste of this traumatized wine, compared to its brother which has lain at home in its château since bottling, may well not be radically different, but if it is a quality wine its development will not be as complete or as advanced. Wines that have a life full of movement will lose something along the way. The only wine which likes heat and being sloshed around is Madeira, which is more or less cooked. It was once used as ballast by ships, as a means of maturing it, so movement can have done it no harm.

I once visited a wine shop which had found cheap premises under a railway arch. As we were tasting and chatting about the virtues of their house Champagne a train went overhead, creating a noise level that made it impossible to speak, and a level of vibration that was almost certainly shaking the quality Bordeaux apart. What it was doing to the Dom Perignon Champagne, stored in open bins in contact with the walls, I dread to think. I didn't buy any wine, and later they stopped selling quality Bordeaux. Some places can injure wine.

The most common kind of storage is metal and wooden racks, which are very useful, but can damage the labels, if bottles are dragged against the metal part and torn. If you want to sell them, torn labels will reduce their price. Plastic sheaths will protect bottles in these conditions, and they will also keep a bottle and its loose label together, should it come off. A common fault is to keep pulling bottles out to look at them. This shakes them about and puts the label at risk each time. Yes, it's all a part of it, and I do it too, but try to separate your drinking wines from your keeping wines, and only admire the drinking ones. Leave the keepers alone. Generally, wine racks should be twelve holes high and/or wide to allow keeping some bottles in dozens.

If you buy fine wines that come in wooden cases you have a dilemma. Say you buy Château Pétrus, the most expensive claret in the world, 1982, the best recent vintage, wouldn't you just like to check that that really is what is in the case before you start dreaming about £5,000 in 2005? You have to be very careful opening the case, because the top planks are tongued and grooved, and if you snap them, you'll have reduced the resale value of the wine. Lever the lid up very carefully, making sure that you bring all the planks up together, and nail back securely afterwards.

Wooden boxes are the most effective storage medium, as they help protect the wine from damage, and they can be stacked up to 10 high. They may be better off the floor, if there is any damp. Christie's have one horror story involving wooden cases kept in a damp cellar, which produced a significant crop of mushrooms all over the wood. 300 cases of the finest Bordeaux, '70s and '75s, were under attack, and £150,000-worth of wine was looking at the wall. Each bottle had to be uncased and individually dipped into a mild disinfectant solution; that's 3,600 bottles. The cases had to be burnt. Quite a job, but the house would have been the next target for the damp. That's the sort of problem some of us might enjoy being able to have, of course. The culprit was the wood from a château.

Cases should be stacked on laths, or some other wooden protector, off the floor, with their heads pointing out, so you can admire their names. Wine racks can be stored on top of cases, although too great a weight may damage the wood.

To get the long view on bottles, old and new, I visited Michael Broadbent MW, doyen of the vintage wine sector, and Head of the Wine Department at Christie's. Over a glass or two of 1839 Madeira – lovely acidity, rich and intensely smooth – I asked him whether he believed there was a breathing through the cork?

'Yes, there is a change of air. The life of a wine depends on the cork. But my theory is that if the wine is good, and it's been kept cool and still, it should be fine even after a hundred years. The cork is crucial. I've come across 200-year-old corks. They've shrunk, and they either become very hard or very soft and spongy.'

The best cellar to have is a cold, damp, Scottish cellar, he believes. Christie's recently sold the contents of a European baron whose cool, dry cellar had made the corks very brittle, so that when they were drawn they crumbled. Even in those circumstances, however, he would prefer not to re-cork.

'The one wine which never seems to have problems with corks is Sauternes, because of the high sugar and glycerine layer on top, it sits like an oil. With very old Sauternes, you tend to push the cork in if you're not careful. You have to get the hooked point of the corkscrew into it and pull it very gently.'

The best system of organizing a cellar he knows of is to have white wine at the bottom and red wine at the top. 'The old-fashioned wooden laths as bins are the most economical. Frankly, wine racks are not cheap, and they also damage the label.

'Seepage is a bit of a mystery. I've seen some very sticky bottles which have a lot of seepage, and yet there has been little ullage [the gap between the wine and the cork]. Vintage Port drips in a cool cellar, but claret doesn't. The only reason why that might happen is because the Port has a wax capsule which may be more porous than the lead ones.'

When to open the bottle, and how long a wine should breathe for has always been a great dilemma. Michael believes there are no hard and fast rules. 'I remember tasting a very old Lafite in America with Elie Rothschild and he said that with very old bottles at the château, 1874 for example, they put the wine into an open pan and give it a bloody good shake. Then they decant it. I was amazed, because everybody always says that you can kill a very old bottle by treating it roughly and opening too soon, but this simply didn't apply in this case. If the wine is very good it will expand in the glass.

'So many people don't allow an old wine to develop; it will often take twenty to forty minutes or up to an hour to develop in the glass alone. Actually when the cork is drawn doesn't make that much difference, because the air doesn't leap in, and even decanting doesn't aerate the wine very much, it's in the glass that the real difference comes.

'It's partly oxidation, but also the convection of air starts the release of flavour and bouquet. Even white Burgundy, which is always drunk far too cold, needs half an hour. Sadly most people drink their white Burgundies from the ice bucket, and their red wines too quickly. Sweet wines don't change in the glass too much, but I always decant them because they look so marvellous in the decanter. Sauvignon Blanc hardly changes in the glass, just slightly, Gewürztraminer and Gamay change not at all, but Chardonnay does. Cabernet Sauvignon and Pinot Noir do, Madeira doesn't.'

Storing and organizing wine: the basics

Marking any open bins where bottles are stored loose in the cellar can be done in various ways, by using marker pens on plastic, neck labels, or even 'Post-it' notes. Tiny round stickers can be stuck onto the top of the capsule, with, 'Ch.X, '83', written on it. There is no best way to mark out and organize your cellar, only a best way for you, your cellar, and the bottles you are storing there.

There is no advantage in having an expensive cellar book, unless it gives you pleasure in itself. Much greater flexibility can be had by using an A4 loose-leaf binder. Wine bought by the unmixed case can be given a page to itself, and single and fewer than twelve bottles can be collected together with other similar bottles on one page. Write the basic label details at the top of the page, e.g. Château X, Graves, 1987. Also write when you bought it, from whom, how much you paid, and the quantity.

How much else you write is up to you. A good idea is to add when you drank the bottles, and the quantity consumed, plus the tally of remaining bottles. Personally, I also think it's a good idea to add with whom you drank the bottle, what you ate with it, and your impressions of the wine and its development. At the time this can seem rather tedious and even obsessive, but if you have bought a few decent bottles, by the time you have finished the last of them, you might like to look back and re-live some of that past pleasure.

Those with a bent for these things can certainly input their cellar into a computer, or even a Psion organizer. I will leave it to those people to work out how best to do it. Otherwise, depending on the amount of wine you have, organize the cellar book in a way that makes your consumption clear, as this is the key to your future buying. One way is to divide and sub-divide regions until you run out of bottles, and the same for vintages, alphabetically.

Think back over the past month: how many bottles did you get through? Count those you took as presents, add those bottles you wished you'd had, and then multiply that by twelve? If that comes to more than fifty, then planning your needs will make sense. Next, break down the pattern: how much good wine, how much plonk? If, say, you reckon on a ratio of 50:50 or 70:30, you can then work out how many bottles of good wine you could mature and improve?

Once you have established your annual consumption, the thing to do is to buy next year's now, and as much of the following year's wine as you can afford.

One aid to the organization of fine wines is to get some square ruled paper and mark it out with however many years seems useful – say five – but if you are buying 'fine' wine, as opposed to 'good' wine that will mature, you will need longer.

	90	91	92	93	94	95	96	97	98	99	00	01	02	03 04 05
Chateau X														(12 bottles)
(a fast maturer)														
Chateau Y														(12 bottles)
(slow)														(12 bottles)

As you drink a bottle, put an 'x' or a '1' in the box for the year in which it was drunk. In this way you can get a clear view of your future needs, and how your stock will develop – whether, for example, you have too much long-term maturing stock, or not enough.

Troubleshooting in a cellar

Firstly, of course, a cellar is simply wherever you store your wine. Ideally you should get a min/max thermometer and a humidity detector. A quick humidity check can be carried out by dampening a sponge and standing it on a plate in the place to be tested. If it's dry in twelve hours or so, the place is not too damp. If the area is too dry you can add some moisture by putting a tray of damp sand into the cellar.

Conversely, dry sand will have the effect of drying the cellar out. Cork will also reduce moisture.

Small draughts are good but big ones are bad. Big draughts lead to larger than desirable swings in temperature. You can test for them by hanging a piece of ribbon, or something similarly light, from the ceiling and seeing if it swings around too much. Waving is bad, occasional rustling, just OK.

Check for vibration by placing a saucer of water on the floor; if there are visible ripples, then vibration is going to be a problem. If you have to live with this, you can minimize the effects by lagging the contact areas. Don't store any wine directly on the floor or against the wall. Put padding under the racks, of sacking, plastic, wood or rubber, and attach the racks to the walls by means of springs or rope.

The key to improvised cellars is heat targeting. By taking readings with your thermometer, identify the relative sources of heat and cold in the cellar, and then insulate your problem area – usually a heat invasion. Do this by laying strips of foil or other insulators against the heat source wall. Make sure you don't inhibit the ability of the 'cold wall' to chill down the ambient temperature by a few vital degrees.

If you've got a big problem with heat, damp or cold, then your only solution is to smother the bottles completely in sawdust.

3

WHERE TO STORE WINE

A flat is not the greatest place to store wine in the long term; sadly, for me, I live in one. Flats have a higher and more even temperature than houses, which often have cold areas and unused parts. But even within a room or small flat there can be radical differences of temperature from one part to another. In this case there is no average temperature, but an ambient temperature, which offers some hotter and some colder edges.

So, you need to ask how hot is your bedroom, how warm under the bed, and how cold the unused fireplace? If the ambient temperature of the room is 72°F, it will usually be 2° hotter than that near the source of heat (e.g. the radiator) and 2° less than that by an outside wall. The kitchen is usually 1° hotter than other rooms and suffers greater swings of temperature. It is therefore a bad place to store wine.

The ideal, of course, is no-work wine storage; the lazy person's cellar. This is not as unlikely as it sounds and is possible in a number of places around the home. Open your eyes, look around you, and you will see places to store wine coming out the walls.

The top non-cellar seven
1. In the loft
2. Under the stairs
3. Under the bed
4. In bedside cabinets
5. In the garage
6. In the wardrobe
7. In the shed

Here are some more, which don't need serious DIY or organization
8. Chest of drawers
9. Filing cabinets
10. Coal hole
11. Behind books
12. On shelves on the walls

Serious DIY
13. Under the floorboards
14. Built into a box room
15. Fireplace

There are also some very bad places to store wine, which will probably kill the wine after only a few months. Most of us, myself included, keep wine there; I mean the kitchen. Only the bathroom is worse, unless you have the sort of insulated cupboards that colour supplement adverts are made of. Other places to avoid are shelves at the top of walls in rooms that are heated a lot – heat rises. Even worse is near a heat source, hot pipes or in contact with the washing machine, where the wine could get shaken up nicely. Other problems lie in wait for those who store a lot of wine at the top or on top of their wardrobe. One day they may find that it all comes down on top of them. Only store one layer of bottles at the top of the wardrobe.

1. The loft
The loft can be the coldest and one of the warmest parts of the house or flat, but the trick is to take advantage of the coldest part of it. If you haven't had your loft insulated, then do so, as this will make it much colder. Oz Clarke used to keep his wine in his loft, covered by blankets which moderate the temperature.

Serious DIY is possible in the loft if you wish to build a platform or box to house some bottles: use contiplas on top, and insulate the bottom with, say, polycarbonate sheets, which you might also use for the walls. Possible plan: 4' × 6' insulating matting attached to a wooden frame, with one side, the north one, uninsulated and open to receive cold from the outside wall. Do take a temperature reading in the winter just in case it is too cold.

2. Under the stairs
This is a popular place to keep wine. It is possible to have wine racks made to measure to fit the space, but it is much better to have double wine racks fitted, if you have the forward space for two bottle depth. They are a commitment though, and not cheap, bearing in mind that they may not fit into another house if you move. Check especially that no horrors lurk in the corners, such as hot-water pipes.

If the under-stair space is open to the hallway, it should be filled in for greater insulation and stability of temperature. This really is an easy job: buy some cheap hardboard, contiplas, or plywood, fit to space, mark out a door, and remove the whole. Cut the door out, attach with hinges and fit. Even cheaper is construction from lengths of board: build them into a wall with backing strips, and use a single piece for the door; fit, and attach some form of latch. It's easy because we are not aiming at an air-tight seal, but one that can be filled in easily and painted over.

3. Under the bed
Too easy to get at? Beds that are just frames are better for storing and retrieving single bottles but are subject to greater temperature varia-

tion than beds with drawers under them. These are ideal in terms of insulation, but difficult to use because to retrieve one bottle means you have to shake them all up. However, this is one of the coolest parts of the bedroom. Drawers are a good place to store twelve bottles of Chateau X which you want to keep for two to three years, and then take them out all together for drinking.

4. Bedside cabinets
These can be very good places to store wine, though not for very many bottles. If the cabinets stand against an outside wall, they will be cool, and are also quite stable environments. Store the wine in a cardboard box. The only general problem with bedroom storage places is that the bedroom is a rather dry room; quality bottles in longish-term storage could be moistened by leaving them in the bathroom for a day or two every now and then.

5. In the garage
Garages can be very cold, but very hot too; any wine stored in the garage needs to be well insulated and also quite safe from accidents; they can so easily be driven over, tipped off shelves, covered in evil-smelling oil or petrol, found by children or stolen by somebody. Bear all these in mind when organizing the garage. The opportunity offered should not be wasted, however, as potentially quite a lot of wine can be stored here.

6. In the shed
Equally cold, if not colder; the shed suffers from the same problems as your garage, but offers more scope to solve them permanently. Wine storage can happily be built into benches and walls, or wedged behind the lawnmower. Some serious DIY is possible here in the manner of the loft micro-room.

7. In the wardrobe
Bearing in mind what was said above about safety and the top shelf, the main chance in wardrobes is at the bottom, which is a good place to store wine, in wooden boxes, cardboard boxes or even milk crates.

At this point, a thought: you will get a lot more out of storing your bottles around you at home, if you first identify what some of these bottles are for; i.e. are they for long-term storage or for drinking up? On that basis, you can begin to organize the different sites for storage in accordance with your plan for drinking, and the ease of access.

8. Chest of drawers
Start with the bottom drawer and work up as far as you can. Bear in mind that if you open one drawer and get it jammed, you are also vibrating the bottles. That's not so bad for big red wines, but whites might do better somewhere else. You can fit cut-down cardboard boxes in the drawer, or, to be more organized, use triangular section

rods on double-sided tape in the floor of the drawer to ensure the bottom layer of bottles is stable, then fit a second layer on top of them.

9. Filing cabinets
Same problem as with the chest of drawers, of course. Not everyone has a filing cabinet at home, either, but if you can buy one cheaply it is a good place to store wine. The cabinet can be locked, it cannot be stolen easily and it is reasonably space efficient. Wine can be stored in the garage or shed and elsewhere in a filing cabinet. Bottles are stored neck on neck (see below for calculations of wine storage in a filing cabinet).

10. In the coal hole
If you have one of these, and don't use coal any more, you are in luck. One coal hole I know is extraordinarily constant in its temperature, remaining 60°F, day and night. Some people also store their cheese in the coal hole, but wines and cheese do not mix in storage.

Security is the key thing here. If the coal hole is accessible to the outside world, make sure it has a strong door and good locks on it. Don't make it airtight; ideally a small gap at the top and bottom of the door will allow for convection and a change of air to prevent the build up of musty smells.

A potential source of trouble in a coal hole is any manhole cover. It leads somewhere, so lift it up and have a look underneath. If there is a big space and things seem pretty secure, any floods should pass you by. Just in case, seal it with a soft, non-setting water sealant, and you should be OK.

11. Behind books
Especially useful if the bookshelves or bookcases stand against an outside wall. Most people have a gap at the front of their bookshelves which is wasted space. Bring the books forward, and lay bottles behind them. Obviously, don't try to lay bottles on top of each other, or disaster will follow. This system is as good as the number of books you own. If you are leaving the bottles here for a while they must be protected from the light, so wrap them in paper or silver foil.

12. On shelves on the wall
Similar to behind books. A large shelving system attached or not to the wall will offer space for a few bottles. This is not going to work among your knick-knacks in the sitting room, but in a spare room or den, or wherever, as many or as few can be stored according to need rather than aesthetics.

For more options see also the next chapter on Serious Cellars, where the Spur shelving system and others are described, all of which would be suitable for wall storage.

13. Under the floorboards

This offers opportunities and difficulties. One idea: useful in a spare room or an area of the floor that is not much walked on, where the boards do not need to be securely re-fitted. Lever the side of the board up using a bolster (a sort of wide chisel). Get more leverage with the claw of a hammer, and using a chisel to keep the board up, work your way along the board.

It may not be pleasant under there, and you may need to clean it up before you put the wine in. Ideally you should remove 2 boards to get more armroom. After reading the next section, replace the board using short nails to ease later removal, also reduce the number of nails.

The second idea: for those who know their floorboards well. The last but one board to the skirting is sometimes not tongue-and-groove as the rest are, being fixed to the last floorboard as shown in the diagram.

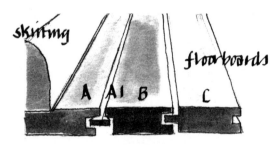

Underneath the floorboards.

In this case, B can be secured to A1, and the corner of B's groove can be cut and B secured to A and C by the same means: dual screw receivers. With the board in situ and B's lower lip removed, drill through into the holding piece, A1, or the joist, having taped the drill to gauge depth into the lower piece of wood. Remove board, tap receivers into board and receiving piece, and then the screw bit and key are used to open and shut the whole assemblage. This is not for those who do not enjoy serious, close-quarters DIY.

A third, equally crazy idea: build a trapdoor! Anyone capable of attempting this will hopefully only need limited guidance. Remove boards, cut the length, having decided on one or two doors, use countersunk hinges, and a countersunk flush ring, and you will have added a feature to the room.

A word about this area: Any bottles stored here should rest on some kind of shelving, because if there is a ceiling below, it will likely be made from plasterboard, which will not necessarily bear the weight. Boxes, laths, and even suspensions from the solid board are possible.

14. Built into a boxroom

This solution is only suitable for those who intend to be long-term residents in the premises. Take a look around your box room or spare room, and ask yourself which is the most important thing to retain its present integrity: the floor or a wall – i.e. do you want to shrink the room horizontally or vertically? The aim is to build a new wall or a floor or floor portion into the room.

The wall Either buy a wine storage unit from a shop or make one yourself. Cover it with insulated hardboard or contiplas, and attach to the wall. You must decide whether you want to have a 'walk-in' or a screen-door.

The floor Build a frame cage from 2 × 1in or larger pieces of timber, and likewise attach covering. Contiplas is very strong and cheap and will reinforce it if it is to be walked on; alternatively, you can turn this into a window seat. Bear in mind that you will not be building more than two bottles deep, so put a double depth wine rack or something you've made yourself in place.

DIYwise, both these jobs are fairly straightforward, and a piece of cake compared to the floorboards options.

15. The fireplace

The fireplace is even easier. You won't be able to store many bottles here, unless you live in the sort of place which is likely to have a cellar anyway; if you want to make it look nice there will be some work, which, frankly, for twelve bottles is not really worth doing.

If you must, here it is: the top of the chimney must be capped, by a cap that will keep out the rain, but not fully sealed. This is a good idea anyway, and it may well have been done already. Put a metal regulator plate with a small trap-door into the chimney shaft and in front either a hardboard or a plastic board, not fully sealed, to allow airflow. It is very important that there be a relatively free flow of air from the outside into the room via the chimney, or a damp problem might arise.

Anyone who doesn't like DIY will have a nightmare during parts of the following chapter where heavy-duty floor treatments will be gone through, but that's enough of that for a while. DIY has its moments, and the pleasure to be gained from it is not universal, but for those on the verge of joining the club, the key pleasure of DIY is in not bodging up a job, but in really knowing what you're going to do before you start. Like the rest of life, DIY needs good contingency planning, or a lot of luck. Choose one route or the other.

Weights and measures; the bottle and its many possibilities

Two Bordeaux bottles (left) and two Burgundy bottles (right) laying down.

Bottle dimensions

	weight	height	width
German	1.23kg	304mm	71mm
	2lb 11½oz	12³⁄₁₆in	2⁷⁄₈in
Bordeaux	1.28kg	284mm	75mm
	2lb 13oz	11³⁄₈in	3in
Champagne	2.63kg	312.5mm	75mm
	3lb 10oz	12½in	3in
Burgundy	1.31kg	292mm	75mm
	2lb 14½oz	11¹¹⁄₁₆in	3in

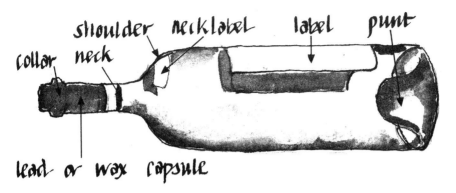

shoulder · neck label · label · punt
collar · neck
lead or wax capsule

The anatomy of a bottle.

Multiple weights Here are the dimensions of some very unpauperish wines that come in wooden cases:

	weight	height	width	depth
1 case 12 bottles Ch. Cheval Blanc	19kg (41lb 12oz)	190mm (7½in)	330mm (13in)	500mm (20in)
1 case 6 magnums Ch. Cheval Blanc	19kg (41lb 12oz)	235mm (9½in)	385mm (15½in)	365mm (14½in)
1 case 12 bottles Grahams Vintage Port	21.5kg (47lb 5oz)	310mm (12½in)	320mm (13in)	400mm (16in)
1 case 12 bottles Taylor Vintage Port	21kg (46lb 3oz)	240mm (9½in)	305mm (12in)	335mm (13½in)
1 solid cardboard box	1.7kg (2lb 6oz)	337.5mm (13½in)	378mm (15⅛in)	280mm (11¼in)
12 free bottles Bordeaux	16.25kg (35lb 13oz)			
12 free bottles Champagne	19.9kg (43lb 13oz)			

Storage on Spur and other flexible shelving systems
Using standard mail-order cardboard boxes, or, as they are known in the trade, cartons, arrangements for stacking are calculated thus:
15½in + 2 × ½in for ventilation spaces = 16½in for the first box, and 15¾in for each further one: So 16½ + 15¾ + 15¾ etc.

For boxes lying on their ends, which is less desirable in terms of access and stability:

Box of 11¼in + 2 × ½in for spaces = 12¼in for the first, 11¾in for each subsequent box. So 12¼ + 11¾ + 11¾in etc.

Lying on side

Heights: box height is 11¼in, plus possible ¹¹⁄₁₆in maximum for shelving material, plus 1in for air space gives about 13in height from the bottom of one shelf to the bottom of shelf above.

Lying on end

Box height is about 15¼in plus possible ¹¹⁄₁₆in for shelving material, plus 1in for air space giving around 17in height from bottom of one shelf to bottom of shelf above.

Neck to neck

Sometimes called the English system or the necking system, the method of storing bottles neck to neck is the most space efficient, thus:

The necking system.

The next layer is laid in the groove of the layer below. The depth above is 19¾ in for Bordeaux bottles, for Champagne, bottom end to end would be 23 in.

This method is ideal for binning various parcels of wine; it would be unwise to try this with different sorts of wines. Historically, the Scottish version of this system was to have bottle lip to bottle lip, with another bottle lying across the necks of the two:

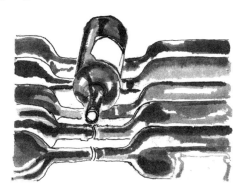

The Scottish system.

The cheapest way

Binning with laths, which are thin lengths of wood, is the cheapest way to store wine, but you do need a lot of bottles and space to make it work, and the commitment to keep them in place for some time. A wine merchant's or château's cellar will be organized in this way. The lath can be any seasoned thin length of wood, roughly 25 × 5mm (1 × ¼in) or whatever you can get.

The floor must be clean. Place two laths on it, and a bottle across them. The next bottle is placed as in the necking system, but with its neck resting on a further lath that is lying on top of the first bottle. Then another lath is placed on the second bottle, and a third on the next in the same way. If there is a flat wall in the area, rest one side of this stack against it. Go as high or as wide as you like. The last bottle on each side is kept in place with a chip of lath or some other stay, but make sure it is tight.

Cheap, cheap, cheap

The next cheapest way to store wine is to go to the local supermarket and get some free boxes. Spirit boxes are strongest. They don't come with dividers inside, but they are good for storing twelve bottles in a kind of informal bin. To start thinking on a larger scale, imagine six of these boxes stacked in the garage or in the cellar – seventy-two bottles more than one a week for a year. That said, cardboard cartons have a disadvantage which is that they are very susceptible to damp. If this is going to be a problem for you, make sure that you change the boxes every so often. A damp, collapsing box is sooner or later going to break some of your bottles. The cheapest way to insulate bottles against cold or heat is to use flattened-out cardboard boxes, news-paper or silver foil.

If you are storing wine in cardboard boxes outside, they shouldn't rest directly on concrete, but rather on wood and/or sacking. The boxes used for mail-order wine are very much better than the ones that supermarkets have in their box dumps, and the difference is in the double-width corrugated board inner dividers, which are sufficiently strong to support a bottle above an empty space. Dimensions are: h. 337.5mm (13½in), w. 387.5mm (15½in), d. 280mm (11¼in).

Assuming those dimensions, a stack of these can be built using wooden frames. The frame can either be lath-type strips, or 2 × 1in timber, nailed or screwed together to form a cage on which the boxes rest. Any such structure should also have diagonal strips to keep the whole stable.

Two boxes on their sides = 13½in high, 30½in wide. Six boxes, plus 1in inclusion of the frame per each height and width of box in the frame, at 3 × 2 boxes: 25in high, 50½in wide. Doubling the dimensions of the horizontal load gives twelve boxes = 144 bottles: 50in high, 101in wide.

The higher and wider you go, the more important the wooden frame becomes as one weak spot in one box could be disastrous. The same timber could also be used to make wooden bins for the bottles directly, without the boxes. Rather than bins as such, it would also be possible to construct single bottle racks, which would be more economical if they were double depth.

I walked round various DIY warehouses to see what they could offer. This is what I found (all prices quoted were current around the time of going to press):

Roofing battens could make a cage: about £2.50 for 1.8m (6ft) lengths, smaller than 2 × 1in.

What you could do: give the wood a coat of wood preservative, after it has had the rough edges taken off. Use rust-proof nails or galvanized screws, preferably twin-fast thread (two threads). David Nye, a DIY expert from B&Q, recommends using contiplas especially as it's so cheap. He doesn't like the idea of using secondhand wood, which although even cheaper may bring infestation into the house with it.

Hole cutter for cutting holes in lath pieces of wood to make neck rests and for storing individual bottles.

The rest should not exceed ¾in in height, and remember that single bottle allowances vary. For general use, bottle allowance should be 3¾in from centre of bottle to centre of bottle.

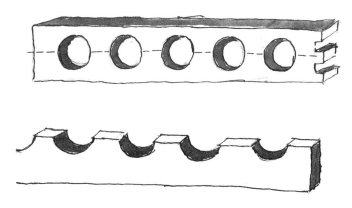

Bottle neck rest.

G clamps are useful for holding together temporary structures or allowing the worried to sleep at night. G clamp capacity 75mm (3in) depth 38mm (1½in) price £2.15.

For very high strength and adjustable clasping across a long or variable surfaces, a **Stanley Web Clamp** is ideal: a webbing band made from a nylon/Terylene mix, rather like a luggage strap, in this case with a metal ratchet adjuster. It is very strong and adjustable, £11.95.

Not every cellar person would think of checking out the garden centre first at a DIY warehouse, but there are some things of interest there. **Pallets** can be used for storing wine. Handle with garden gloves and sanitize before bringing into the house. It's not worth buying pallets, but if you can get them free they are quite useful. They all theoretically belong to someone, but in many cases that was a long time ago. There are three basic sizes:

600 × 787.5 × 130mm (24 × 31½ × 5¼in), interior height 106mm (4¼in)

980 × 1155 × 162.5mm (39¼ × 46¼ × 6½in), interior height 93mm (3¾in)

1225 × 1175 × 143mm (49 × 47 × 5¾in), interior height 100mm (4in)

There are two designs, open and closed. Closed pallets are not ideal and have two open sides and two closed sides. The open ones have four open sides. Pallets are usually used to rest things on, of course, but for our purposes they can be used to rest bottles *in*. Pallets are not space-efficient, and ideally should stand in the middle of an area, to be accessible on two or four sides for bottles.

Garden trellises are perfect in design and quite cheap. They come in three 'strengths', but only use the strongest, which is 31 × 18mm (1¼ × ¾in). We can use also a novel form of calculation which is Cost of Bottle Stored – cbs – the price of the object divided by the number of bottles it can hold. It all helps to liven things up a bit.

Specifications:

2 × 180 × 300mm (6 × 1ft) @ 2 × 2 holes @ £4.98 = 40p CBS

2 × 180 × 600mm (6 × 2ft) @ 12 × 4 holes @ £7.59 = 31p CBS

2 × 180 × 900mm (6 × 3ft) @ 12 × 6 holes @ £9.75 = 27p CBS

Construction involves two trellises and approximately 14.3cm (5¾in) centre of hole to centre, hoping that the bases of the bottles will rest against a wall or strip of hardboard. The first trellis can stand on a lath, to raise the neck of the bottle, with the two planes joined by other pieces of wood. Hole size is a little big, at 112.5 × 112.5mm (4½ × 4½in). It might be possible to build a double-depth trellis construction with two bottles neck against neck, but this might be pushing frugality beyond the realms of safety. Still, a really good CBS of 20p is obtained by using three of the largest trellises. Another option would be to use them horizontally, along the floor, in an otherwise difficult area.

Ventilator units: without moving parts, telescopic wall unit

Adapt-A-Vent, £12.95

Ventilator fitted to a wall or door, £7.95

Just about the most useful thing possible is a **combined thermometer and humidity meter**, £3.75.

For serious construction, **sawn timber**:

3.7 × 18mm (1½ × ¾in) pack of ten, × 2.4m (7ft 10in) long, £9.45

5 × 25mm (2 × 1in) pack of ten, × 2.4m (7ft 10in) long, £10.25

Homebase DIY warehouse guarantees that 'for every tree cut, one or two seedlings are planted or four to eight seeds sown, and the forest managed'.

Insulation: especially useful in flats, insulation is important to limit the extremes of temperature that attack wine. Total isolation can be achieved by using cork tile (six tiles for £2.49) on a flat surface, perhaps combined with metal foil; a large part of what we are trying to achieve is also the targeting of hot spots and cold spots to the advantage of the wine. Some other things:

Twill ceiling tiles,

20 × 500mm × 500mm, flame retardant, £8.29

25 × 300mm × 300mm, £2.69

If you need more flexibility or to cover irregular surface areas, use rolls of wall and ceiling veneer:

length, 9140mm (30ft), £4.99

width, 600mm (23½in)

thickness, 2mm

thickness, 7mm, £9.35

If damp is a potential problem, exclude it with polythene damproof film, 4m (13ft 4in) wide, 22p per metre, or to provide insulation as well, the 'popper' air pocket plastic sheeting, 89p per metre.

If your specific problem is that you want to store a number of bottles for the same length of time, then one solution may be to create a little microclimate for them, to give them their own room. Ariel cordux PVC sheeting may be the thing; it is usually used for greenhouse roofing and is corrugated to just the right width for a Bordeaux bottle to fit snugly into. It can be added to any of the 'off the shelf' systems. The cost of a sheet of 'standard' 1.8 × 0.8m (6ft × 2ft in) is £6.25. This cannot allow for individual bottles to be taken out, but this facility is available if wooden laths are added between sheets. The sheeting is cut into 5in widths and lain on the bottles, the bottom layer fixed to the bottom surface. Guttering can also be used in this way, and is a perfect receptacle for a Bordeaux bottle, but is not cheap.

Also on the expensive side is Twin Wall polycarbonate, 240 × 60 × 9mm (8ft × 2ft × ⅜in) at £19.99, but useful where protective strength, the passage of light, and high insulation is required.

Another way to divide bottles, as we saw in a chest of drawers, is by using triangular mouldings or quadrants, cut into 125mm (5in) strips and tacked or taped down.

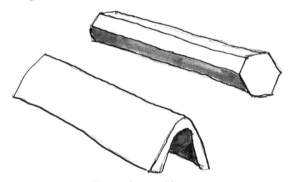

Triangular mouldings.

A useful gadget is the Sellotape Condensation Absorber, usable for two to three months; large £4.99; small £1.75. This would be useful during the conversion of an area with a damp problem into a cellar.

4

SERIOUS CELLARS

I f DIY on a large scale is not for you, I suggest that you throw a little more money at problems, and buy off-the-shelf shelving, with only a little self-assembly or screwing things into walls to be done.

Shelving

Let's start with the most basic shelving system – Spur steel adjustable shelving. This carries with it several considerations. Firstly, don't buy a cheaper, less sturdy system, unless you definitely intend to store only a couple of cases. Secondly, the system is only as strong as the wall the upright is screwed onto. A third thing to bear in mind is that the maximum gap, centre upright to centre upright should be two feet. The good thing about this system is that it is widely available, and quite cheap.

Spur shelving.

A bracket is slotted into the upright and, ideally, a shelf is screwed onto the bracket. The brackets should be 220mm (9in), which gives a weight tolerance of 85kg (187lb), or 270mm (10½in) which gives a weight tolerance of 75kg (165lb).

This means that the bracket will support the weight as an evenly distributed maximum. Thus 270mm (10½in) brackets will support 150kg (330lb), well in excess of the weight of two cartons of Bordeaux plus shelving. It's not a good idea to cheesepare on the quality of the shelving, because a few pounds saved could be more than eaten up by one disaster or minor miscalculation.

The uprights come in different lengths, up to 2400mm (94in), although most DIY warehouses stock up to 1980mm (78in). At B&Q the 78in uprights cost £7.49 each × 2 = £14.98p. Our 325mm (13in) cartons plus shelving and gap fit snugly six times into that 1980mm (78in) although it might be wise to be less greedy and allow for five shelves, allowing us 387mm (15½in) for each shelf.

2 × 5 brackets, 262mm (10½in), @ £1.79 each = £17.90, plus the cost of conti board for five shelves, 300mm (12in) wide, 650mm (26in) long, say £15 equals total cost of £47.88, to store 120 bottles, giving a 39p cbs. Not the cheapest, but very flexible, quite space efficient, and accessible.

Next up the ladder is free-standing industrial shelving, more desirable for some because it can be taken with you when you move. Free-standing units give the impression of being sturdier than attached ones, like the Spur, but that is a fallacy. The Spur directs the force of its load into the wall, hence the need for secure wall attachments; but the free-standing unit is also free-load-bearing – it stands or falls under its own construction. Add to its security by securing it to a wall or some other support, and try to apply a diagonal strip or beam.

Cost of industrial steel shelving at B&Q with four shelves is, Height: 1625mm (65in); width: 787.5mm (31½in); depth: 300mm (12in) – £16.10p.
Supplementary packs of two shelves are available at £6.99, but this is a bad deal when the whole unit is on sale at around £9.99. Four shelves offer 400mm (16in) of vertical space, three times over, while eight shelves offer 200mm (8in) which could allow for the storage of bottles out of their cartons, in which case the structure must be anchored to the wall, and some of the side filled in by hardboard, screwed or clipped. Given the variations possible here, it is difficult to calculate a cbs for it, but however you choose to organize it, it will be quite cheap.

A stronger version of the same idea, and used now by the Wine Society at their new mega-cellars in Stevenage is Dexion Racking. This method of racking, or binning if you have the bottles loose, is not cheap to copy in your own home if you buy it new, but after the lath method it is probably the most space-efficient storage system. You will also sleep at night without the fear of being woken by the sound of breaking glass: it is strong. Fortunately, although it is a large financial commitment, it is easily collapsible and mobile. The Wine

Society's size of bin to store twenty-four bottles, neck on neck, is 12in × 15in internal space.

However, in most towns and in all cities there is somewhere that sells second-hand office equipment including Dexion Racking, often very cheaply, and even more cheaply for cash. £25 per 1.8 × 3.6m (6 × 12ft) bay of racking is about average in London.

Another solution is if you know someone who works for a large organization such as British Gas, British Telecom, the Post Office, or such like. Many large companies have special departments which will sell redundant office equipment to employees very cheaply. Ask your friends.

On to different kinds of shelving, on the whole less sturdy, but often better looking, so if you are forced to have them on view, they may suit you better; they are also easily buyable, if IKEA or Habitat have a store near you. They each stock variations of the same design which are of interest to us. One is good on price and stability, the other is useful as a specific problem solver.

Pine
Habitat's cheapest pine shelving system is appropriately called Utility
    h – 1700mm (67in)
    w – 750mm (29½in)
    d – 300mm (12in)
giving four shelves @ £32.50p, with the same space again as an Extension @ £24.50p = £57. The space totals are:
    h – 1700mm (67in)
    w – 1500mm (59in)
    d – 300mm (12in).

Sadly Habitat do not give weight tolerances for their units beyond saying that they are built for 'everyday loads', whatever these may be. However, a middle way between caution and greed suggests three cartons per 150cm (60in) shelf, across the unit and the extension, giving twelve cartons, with 144 bottles = 39p CBS. Storing wine racks on these shelves would be stretching the limits rather, as the racks themselves are quite heavy.

IKEA's basic pine unit, actually made from spruce, is called Sten, and has three interior shelves for £19.70, with £3 for an extra shelf = £22.70 (cheaper).
    h – 1740mm (68½in)
    w – 890mm (35in)
    d – 310mm (12in).

IKEA give weight tolerances for Sten as 250kg (113lb 9½oz) evenly spread – i.e. not all on one shelf. This is OK. Allowing for 50kg (22lb 11oz) grace, and even storing heavier wooden cases only, that would still allow you ten cases, or 120 bottles, giving an 18p CBS – very cheap indeed.

The great benefit of these systems is mobility, ease of establishment and flexibility. Sten actually comes with its own bottle rack, in the form of triangular section dividers; actually very poor value at £4.95 for eight bottles which gives 61p CBS. You could make them a lot more cheaply, or simply buy one and stack bottles two or three, or more high on that one shelf, filling in the side as you go.

Along with these benefits is one other; the ease with which they can be adapted: looked at another way, both these pine units can also be seen as skeleton wine cupboards.

Here's how: buy some hardboard and nail or screw it onto the pine frame, back and sides, or leave the cold wall free. You then have the option to store bottles without cases, or in cases. Caution advises that the whole structure should be anchored to the wall.

Doors can be:
- on traditional hinges, made from plywood
- held closed with magnets
- replaced by DIY roller blinds, if appropriate

None of these options takes account of the location of your cellar, and you will have to adapt it to the temperature you are trying to achieve. Taping up the joins will keep out the light, and heavy insulation material will control the temperature. Preservation of the wood is desirable, especially if the unit may be subject to damp. Use varnish, or the hugely pauperish might like to use cooking oil. Three coats, dried for a week will preserve the wood – but don't use best olive oil.

On price and flexibility these systems are hard to beat, but they are not fantastically strong. You can think about building something similar yourself, from stronger timber, to increase the specifications; ideally visit a friend who has one already, and take it apart, or just visit the showroom and take your tape measure. It's really very easy, and you will also be building a stronger structure to fit your best spot.

Not ideal, but filling a need for some people, are the wire-mesh systems both IKEA and Habitat offer, and which look like beaten-out shopping trolleys. They are stylish and allow for the maximum amount of light to pass through the storage area. This means the wine itself must be secured from the light. Ideal for displaying fancy wooden cases.

Habitat's system is called Mesh, a chromed metal unit with adjustable shelves. Again, Habitat do not give a weight tolerance, although for IKEA's version, this is 200kg (91lb), and it is probably similar for Habitat's:

h – 1870mm (74in)
w – 820mm (32¼in)
d – 380mm (15in)

cost £89.99p, extension available. If you wanted to store wooden cases, allowing 25 kilos grace, you could store nine, giving you 108 bottles, and 83p CBS. Not cheap, but pretty.

IKEA's version is called Peter, and is costed at £17 for side units ×2, and £10 per shelf ×5 = £84 total.

Neither of these systems is cheap, nor are they ideal for storing large amounts of wine, but if you must store wine in a domestic environment, they are not bad.

Small scale
The safest way to store wine is in wine racks, those basic structures of wood and metal. We have seen that they have their drawbacks, with their trick of tearing labels, but they are solid, and fairly adaptable. Looking at our two stores again, Habitat offer:

30 bottle rack at £10.99 = 36p CBS
16 bottle rack at £6.50 = 40p CBS
12 bottle rack at £5.99p = 50p CBS
Aluminium wine rack:
25 bottles at £8.50 = 34p CBS
50 bottles at £13.99 = 28p CBS

With all the racks, the number of bottles stored depends on which way you place the rack: 30 bottles means the rack is on its long side, otherwise the total is 28; both totals also take advantage of the top four or six places, outside the rack; using these adds 50mm (2in) to the top dimension of the rack.

IKEA offer surprisingly little by way of racks, but what they do, they do well:

Magasin, all pine, 24 bottles at £3.75 = 14p CBS; exceptional value.

Some wine retailers themselves also offer wine racks, and some others also offer a made-to-measure service, Majestic offering a double depth version. A look in the back of *Decanter* and *Wine* magazines will also give you some addresses of makers of wine racks. One example is A. & W. Moore, 222 Mansfield Road, Nottingham, NG7 2BU (Tel: 0602-607012):

30 bottles (24 holes) at £10.75p = 35p CBS
56 bottles (48 holes) at £19.65p = 35p CBS

The main thing to bear in mind is that where a single-bottle depth wine rack will fit, quite often a double depth one will also fit, doubling your storage, and lowering your costs.

A lot of money

We leave the spare thin world of making do and cobbling together, to enter the fragrant world of serious spending power. If you've got it, you might as well spend it on something worthwhile. Life is short, but wine is long, to maul a phrase. If you've got several hundreds or thousands of pounds to spend on your fancy then this is for you. Everyone else should read this sitting down with a glass in hand. This is how to have heaven on your bit of the earth: here comes the Spiral Cellar, over 3,000 built in France, they claim, and yours starting at £2,038, plus VAT (= £2,343.70). This stores 378/432 bottles, which at best gives us £5.42 CBS, not the bargain of the year. These figures also do not take into account the fact that you have to pay more to have it fitted; employing two men for four or five days. Cost? Around £400, depending on where you live; total, £3,154, which gives £7.30 CBS. Much larger versions are available, storing up to 1,600 bottles, for a basic cost of £3,500, excluding VAT.

You have to start with a very large hole, which produces three skips worth of dirt. You can dig this hole into your garage or into one of your downstairs rooms, and a lot of concrete goes into the hole, which, of course, has to be mixed somewhere, and dropped *en route* in many other places. The business end of a Spiral Cellar is a series of brick-type things which interlock and create a sort of spiral staircase, and the bottles are fitted inside the vacant areas. It's ideal in the sense that you do not lose any space, and only worms will feel the downside of it being installed. It is also tornado-proof, apparently a big sales pitch in the US. You and your wine could also survive a nuclear holocaust. Available from Spiral Cellars, The Wines, Hardwick Close, Knott Park, Oxshott, Surrey K22 0HZ (Tel: 0372-842692).

A little more financially accessible is the Eurocave, basically a fridge. Model 210E costs £989, and holds 210 bottles = £4.70 CBS, plus electricity. These machines are quite sophisticated in that some can offer three different temperatures, and are fairly secure. Once you have made the capital investment, you can reap the benefits for years to come. Available from IFM, Martock Business Park, Great Western Road, Martock, Somerset (Tel: 0935-826333).

Converting your cellar

If you are lucky enough to have a cellar, then make the most of your good fortune and convert it into a wine cellar. Here's how:

- Clean it out
- Install a light
- Seal the walls and floor against moisture
- Put in racks and storage

1. Collect the rubbish and throw it away. Give the place a good clean, but don't use any smelly cleaners, and wipe up the water or some of it will stay in the atmosphere.

2. Lights. The cable you'll need is two core and earth, size 1.00mm. Measure and buy more than you think you'll need. At this stage, you will either know what to do next, or you should get an electrician in to do it. Connecting electric cable to fuse boxes is something that it is a very bad idea to get wrong. If you haven't done it before, it is a lot better to watch someone else do it before you attempt it yourself.

3. Having got some light on the subject you will likely find that there are some nasty little problems you hadn't noticed before, like cracks, or 'organic' growth. Plants are symptoms of a damp problem. Brush them off using a stiff brush, but protect your eyes and face. Mix 1 part bleach to 4 parts water and cover the affected area, washing it into the cracks.

Damp-proofing
If the cellar is suffering from penetrating or rising damp, then this basic sealing will not be sufficient. Install a ventilator now.

Penetrating damp is due to moisture getting into the house during wet weather; you'll know because it only happens during or after rain, and will appear as damp patches and stains.

Rising damp comes up from the ground, and is not being stopped by a damp-proof membrane (DMP), usually linked to the damp-proof course (DPC) in the walls. This is really bad news as this is a big job to put right and only the really gifted amateur should start on it. But hopefully none of these problems have been visited on you.

If there are cracks in the concrete floor at different levels, this is due to settlement of the sub-base, so call in the local Building Control Officer. Hopefully this will not be the case. Clean the crack of loose material and open up the narrow parts. Prepare with one part binding agent, five parts water, and allow to dry. To fill in the crack use three parts sand to one part ready-mixed quick-setting cement, mixed with equal parts of bonding agent and water. Apply with a trowel, pressing in well.

The worst scenario of all is having to lay a whole new cellar floor. This is not a difficult job but it is a very big one. Do it yourself only if you really have to or want to. Above all take professional advice before you start.

Your cellar may be damper than you think, so the first thing to do is to dry it out. A blow heater will do fine. Clean out the holes and cracks in the wall and floor, and wash them thoroughly with soapy water to cut through any grease, then clean them out using a chisel. Prime with a coat of urethane, leave for one hour, and then fill in with six parts sand, one part cement, and urethane to produce a sticky paste. It is possible to use just normal filler or cement, but remember that the most common problem in cellars is damp, and so our aim must be to lock creeping moisture out as much as possible.

Cover the floor with four coats of urethane, using a broom, and leave two to three hours between each coat; leave to dry for two days. Use the same treatment for the walls. Where intrusive damp is more of a problem, you may need to dry-line the walls. Remove old plaster and clean up the brick work then cover with a thin coat of mortar, and smooth it out. Paint on two coats of bitumen, wipe dry sand into it to help bind the coats. Finally plaster the walls.

Last of all: introduce secure locks to the doors and windows that open to the cellar, then you're ready to start.

5

REAL CELLARS

Different people have different cellar opportunities and needs. It is time we looked at some.

HM The Queen

The most serious social occasions when wine is served are the state banquets held at Buckingham Palace for foreign dignitaries. If you had been in the right place on 16 April 1985, at the dinner for Malawi, you could have drunk Ch. Ducru-Beaucaillou 1971: not bad. Some other offerings of interest: Taylor and Grahams 1966, Lanson and Bollinger 1976, Clos de Vougeot 1968 (I wonder whose?) and Ch. Talbot 1976.

The years give the game away. All these wines are served at perfect maturity – lucky state banqueters. Needless to say, the atmosphere, the details that surround these occasions and, indeed the Royal Cellars themselves, are seriously out of bounds. Strangely, 'they' are unwilling even to reveal how the cellars are organized.

However I am able to tell you what was drunk at the two recent weddings. Charles and Diana sipped Krug '69 with their wedding breakfast. At Andy and Fergie's bash, Krug '73 was served as an apéritif, and Bollinger '66 with the wedding breakfast.

How a wine gets into the cellar at Buckingham Palace is a matter of semi-secrecy. All those wine merchants who hold a Royal Warrant supply a range of wines every now and then for a blind tasting held by a small group of favoured merchants, and a body of wine is chosen. Not to get a wine chosen from three successive tastings apparently means loss of the Warrant.

The range of wine served at Buckingham Palace banquets is very diverse indeed, within certain constraints. Among the Ports, only the finest are offered – Taylor, Graham, Dow, and very mature. The

STATE BANQUET

IN HONOUR OF

THE LIFE PRESIDENT

OF

THE REPUBLIC OF MALAWI

WINDSOR CASTLE

TUESDAY, 16th APRIL, 1985

Menu

Consommé Sévigné

———

Suprême de Turbot Dugléré

———

Selle d'Agneau Sarah Bernhardt
Chou-fleur Mornay
Purée de Carottes
Pommes Fondantes

———

Salade

———

Bombe Glacée Coppelia

Les Vins

Fino La Ina
Carr Taylor 1982
Chateau Ducru-Beaucaillou 1971
Lanson 1976
Graham 1966

STATE BANQUET
IN HONOUR OF

THE KING AND QUEEN
OF
SPAIN

WINDSOR CASTLE
TUESDAY, 22nd APRIL, 1986

Menu
Crème Solferino

———

Filet de Turbot Fécampoise

———

Selle d'Agneau Madère
Chou-fleur Mornay
Purée d'Epinards
Pommes Cretan

———

Salade

———

Bombe Glacée Rothschild

Les Vins
Amontillado Fine Old
Hochheimer Kirchenstück Spätlese 1982
Imperial Gran Reserva CVNE 1973
Bollinger 1976
Quinta do Noval 1966

clarets are not first growths but some very good names; fine but not the finest. The Champagne is a treat, but leaving aside the very drinkable La Ina, the really interesting section of wines is the German one. It is said, and we cannot really know, that the Queen is partial to a glass of German wine (usually only ever one). Like Queen Victoria, who enjoyed a drop of Hock, the Queen likes to keep up a vinous solidarity with her German roots. Among her subjects today there is what I find to be a depressing lack of interest in fine German wines, so long may she plug away on their behalf. It was also a nice thought to have 1973 CVNE Rioja for 'the Spains', but it wasn't the first choice. Before the banquet, the Palace tried to get sufficient quantities of Vega Sicilia, Spain's greatest wine and as expensive as it is rare, but even they couldn't get hold of enough, so they went for the CVNE instead.

Jancis

From the Queen of England, to the queen of wine: Jancis Robinson. Jancis has done it all, the first wine journalist to become an MW – the highest wine qualification – the first wine programme on TV, a whole series of definitive books; but also owner of one of the most disorganized cellars I have seen. Odd but charming.

At her home in the country she has two wine-storage areas: in the

Jancis Robinson.

basement under the stairs she has a double-depth wine rack, and at the back of the house, she has what she described as a 'lean-to' overlooked by a large window.

The wine rack is very disorganized, but that is the way she prefers it. The excitement lies in not knowing what she will pull out next, and she's happy to spend ten minutes every evening deciding what to drink. She has caught the browsing bug badly, but then she also has very interesting wines to browse over. Beside the main wine rack, there is a magnum rack, and on the other side there is the Champagne; 'yes, I always keep my Champagne for a while, even non-vintage'.

The life of a prominent wine writer must be many people's dream, with bottles arriving thick and fast at the door. 'I get sent a lot of bottles to be tested, small groups of which stand beside this rack. Sometimes I think I should stand outside and say "no" to the postman, "take them back, take them back". And then they sit there, looking rather forlornly at you. But it's rare that one of these bottles will be the one we want to drink that evening. After I've tried a few I tend to give them away, or, in the end I just have to pour them down the sink. That's sad. I once had to pour fifty bottles down the sink.'

This is Jancis's 'problem'; 'as time goes on, the more I regret buying anything but the best.' Her husband, Nick Lander, who made L'Escargot famous in Soho's restaurant land, and she are obviously never short of a bottle or two to drink, so then the criterion of pure drinking pleasure takes over. Jancis is not only the most successful wine journalist, she is also one of the luckiest. 'There's usually never any shortage of things to drink, so you get to the situation when you would like to drink something stunning.'

In financial terms she also thinks that buying wine for investment makes a lot more sense if you stick to the top quality ones; the best wines increase in value at a faster rate than the lesser ones. Her lack of a real cellar is her great regret, but some new neighbours have recently moved in and have made some inviting noises about offering the use of theirs. Until then she is stuck with the lean-to.

It's around 1.2m (4ft) wide widening to about 1.5m (5ft), and about 3.3m (11ft) long. That sounds quite a reasonable size, but it is very underused because most of the wine is stored on the floor in cases and cartons, illustrating the fact that floor storage takes up space, while wall storage creates it. She has identified her own problems: 'It's very difficult to rotate stock, but we did manage to put the Port in first, so it's stuck at the bottom. No, we don't exactly have a cellarbook.'

On the right-hand wall is a large wine rack for around fifty bottles, and this houses some of her 'mistakes'. 'I've got two cases of Ch. Rahoul [Graves] 1983, which I regret very much, it's such a puny wine. I think I bought it on someone else's recommendation.' One of the keys to successful buying is never to buy a case of something you haven't tasted yourself; a few bottles, yes, but no more.

'We've got a lot of Hunter Valley Semillon, which we love when it's mature.' [Try Rothbury Estate, Rosemount, and also Peter Lehmann, and Berri Estates, outside the Hunter Valley.] We pondered a great variety of bottles in the racks, with quite a few German ones. 'With the price they are at auction, it really pays to buy the best, like von Schubert, or J J Prüm.' The excitement of discovery is what makes fiddling with open wine racks fun, especially if, by chance you find yourself looking at a bottle of Ch. Pétrus 1982, picked up quite at random, worth £250. 'My only bottle. The problem with Pétrus is that it's delicious mature or immature.

'One bit of advice I would give is that when you see a good vintage, really pounce on it, and bear in mind that you are not buying for one year. For example, the Italian '85s [see special section in the next chapter] are so good. Guigal '85s also from the Rhône, actually most of the Côtes du Rhône '85s are very good to latch onto. Another pouncer is Raveneau Chablis.

'Likewise, a lot of people, myself included, overbought '82 and '83 Bordeaux. I don't regret the '82s, but the '83 is a patchy vintage. Fortunately my first daughter was born in '82 so we bought some wine for her, although that is in bond. I've currently got some '87s on order, they're quite cheap at the moment; that's another tip, if you want to get some famous names into your cellar, the '87s are a good buy, and they'll drink quite soon.'

Her 'number one' tip is always to buy the best quality you can afford, because later, you won't regret it.

She also likes doing little experiments, and at the moment is keeping bottles of Beaujolais Nouveau, 'just to see what happens to it'. Every now and then her husband will give her a blind tasting from among the bottles in the larger rack. 'Yes, that's very useful, and it's good practice, but I love the pleasure of pottering round the rack so much that I tend to resist. There are so many good wines.'

Jancis would admit that her cellar needs radical re-organization. What she needs is Spur shelves all along the outside wall. The window to the kitchen-diner has a large bay from the cellar, and a Habitat or IKEA wire shelf unit would fit well there, displaying the cases, and not cutting down on the light coming into the kitchen. The far wall could also have high-density storage, with Dexion Racking.

Boris, from the *Financial Times*

The advantages of buying a lot of wine during a period of unusual financial liquidity, is exemplified by the case of Boris, who writes for a number of papers, including the *FT*.

Boris buys 'here and there', dropping into Christie's and Sotheby's to put in the odd low bid. Sometimes he gets a bargain, but mostly he doesn't. One was a case of Magnums of Cos d'Estournel '82, one of his buys in 1986, his big year: cost then £170, price today, about £270.

Like Jancis, Boris's first daughter was born in 1982, so he bought her Ch. Mouton-Rothschild. That was the first time he had bought really good wine. Lucky girl.

During 1986, Boris estimates he spent somewhere in the region of £6,000 on wine, which he did in lieu of a pension plan. 'I've taken out the pension plan since, but I calculate that so far the wine is appreciating faster, by around 40 per cent.' He was buying two or three cases a month in '86, some fine wines, others drinkable sooner. Essentially he was trying to put down enough wine to start him off, before the costs of a family became too big to allow that luxury. Since then he has cut back very much, and now buys only occasionally to extend the range of his cellar; he is most interested in building up his Italian wines.

His tip for filling out an Italian collection is to trawl the Italian delicatessens in search of undervalued bottles, which often stay at the same price for some time. Currently he is buying Pio Cesare Barolo, 1982, from Camisa in Old Compton Street in London's Soho, at £6 a bottle. He may have bought it all up by the time you read this, however. His cellar is primarily a drinker's cellar, and he is happy to buy and keep single bottles, that are of no interest to investors. They always sell at a discount, and are often included in mixed cases.

The construction of his cellar is basic; it is long and thin, with no damp. One wall is covered with wine racks, and on the other side, cases are stacked two or three high with other smaller racks on top of them. It is simple and practical.

Don, who had his garden dug up

Don Philpot is a well known food and wine writer who started collecting bottles in the early '70s, and today finds that he has over 600. Fairly early on he decided that his affection was not going to be a flash in the pan and so he decided to make a commitment to house it properly. The only practical site for a proper, big cellar was to cut into a small 'cliff' in his garden. He got some horrifying quotes, and thought that he could do it cheaper himself, and saved 80 per cent of the cost. Today he has a 3.6 × 2.4m (12 × 8ft) walk-in cellar with humidity controls and a 6-inch double door.

Construction: dig out the earth. You will need to lay 250mm (10in) of cement, next polythene sheeting, then bricks, across all the surfaces. The cement must be a minimum of 9in thick to give stability of temperature; the polythene sheeting and the bricks added a water-proof layer and a porous layer, respectively. The size gives Don a potential 2,000-bottle capacity and he has gone on, in true pauper style, to save further money by his use of filing cabinets to store wine. Averaging twenty-two bottles per drawer, a battered second-hand four-drawer cabinet costing, say, £20, will hold eighty-eight bottles and give a cbs of 22p. The obvious disadvantage of storing wine in a filing cabinet is that you disturb all the bottles in the drawer when you open and close it, so you have to be quite organized about it.

Some of Don's favourite buys by the case:
Châteauneuf-du-Pape, Domaine du Père Caboche, 1979, was £50, now £96.
Domaine de Gaillat, Graves, 1982, was £50, now £72.
Ch. Chicane, Graves, 1983, was £50, now £75.

A doctor says

Dr Louis Hughes is a well-known doctor and wine lover, who has pursued his love through many avenues. He is the ex-Chairman of the Wine and Food Society, wine buyer for the Savile Club, on the wine panel for the Apothecaries' Livery Company, and is involved in many smaller, informal wine groups.

Like Don, Louis went for a big solution to the problem of where to store his wine. 'I had a cellar dug, and used this so called "water-proof" cement. It leaks, of course, so we had to make the floor sloping, and the water runs down to the drain in the corner, where there's a high pressure pump to take it out. Even so, that's not enough sometimes, and I have to use a de-humidifier to take more out the atmosphere, so the corks won't be drying out in here. Even though from the construction point of view it's a disaster, it actually works fine.'

The cellar is roughly 4.2 × 2.4m (14 × 8ft) and is organized in a very logical way, based on three layers, starting with bins for loose bottles at the bottom, then wooden cases, and wine racks on top. The bins store 54 bottles each, double depth, when full, six high and five across and Louis uses a cross-piece from a wooden case to stabilize the load. For this neck-on-neck system to work properly, the floor must be flat. The cases stand two high.

Dr Louis Hughes.

The system: 'Every New Year's Day I more or less spend the day in the cellar. I open the cases which are ready for drinking and load them into the bins. Those wines which have been in the bins and are rather reduced, then go up into the racks. That's the idea, anyway.'

The boxes are fairly easily removed by jemmying up the rack above, and then removing the box. He uses neck labels on the bottles in the racks, which show the wine and the vintage, e.g. La Lagune, '78. It is a lot of work to put the labels on, but once you've got them on there's really no excuse to keep picking up the bottles, so it's a good idea on that basis.

Useful cellar accessories:
- Pritstick glue, for sticking labels back on
- screwdrivers, general use
- jemmy, to open and move cases
- formica strips, for writing the contents of bins on with a dry pen, which wipes clean after the bin has been changed around
- a small exercise book, in which he writes down everything he takes from the cellar, and eventually transfers to a cellar book he keeps elsewhere. 'An expensive cellarbook is a

waste of money, and you change your system so many times that I prefer the flexibility of a loose-leaf file.'

Louis's cellar is nicely decorated. He has some antique wine labels and bin numbers. His son, Christopher, makes ceramic cellar labels with wine names on them, e.g. Burgundy, Claret, Sauternes, Port and Champagne available at £3.50, from Christopher Hughes, c/o 99 Harley Street, London W1. Box ends from delicious names and vintages decorate the other walls.

Buys and tips: Louis's cellar is not the most pauperish, but like anyone else he sees value for money as the guiding principle. He recommends: 'Don't miss a good Burgundy vintage. Although they are expensive, it's worth buying into because they only happen every five years or so, so you should spend four or five years-worth of "Burgundy money" on buying them.

'Do the same, but less intensively with Bordeaux. But buying *en primeur* is becoming less attractive at the moment because there's a lot of good Bordeaux around. Prices are not moving up as fast as they used to. The only reason to buy *en primeur* these days is if you want a particular property.'

He doesn't cellar white wine, except Sauternes, preferring to buy and drink. Above all, he recommends 'taste, and taste some more, and more, as much as you can, and home-in on the things you like'. The things he likes, apart from Bordeaux and Burgundy, are southern French wines, from the Rhône and from Provence. He was an early buyer of Mas de Daumas Gassac, 'the Latour of the Languedoc', and another favourite is Ch. d'Aix-en-Provence (1975). For real value he believes Australia is hard to beat and he thinks that Chile will be a good source of value wine in the future. Two of his most unusual wines are from California, Louis Martini Mountain Cabernet 1958, and Inglenook 1958. Currently he is drinking delicious half bottles of Clos du Marquis (St Julien) 1983. He always keeps his Champagne at least two years, whether it's Krug or supermarket non-vintage.

A doctor's prescription: Louis and his family drink at least one bottle of red wine a day with dinner, and one red and one white on Fridays. 'On average we go through 1 case a week.' But he is not a spirits man. 'I've got duty-frees I bought fifteen years ago in the cabinet. I'm rather against spirits, and it's often the gin before, or the Cognac after a meal that puts you over the limit. I never drink before eating, I usually have a Pink Angostura, tonic water and ice. Spirits on an empty stomach are absorbed very fast into the bloodstream, that's the problem.

'People get terribly serious about wine, but it is such good fun. If it's not fun, it's not worth doing.'

6

WHICH WINE TO STORE

In this chapter we shall review those areas of world production which produce wines which are generally available and that are worth keeping. We start with France, still the biggest supplier of wine to the UK, and by far the biggest supplier of quality wines.

Apart from certain grape varieties, France has also given the world a classification system that has been widely imitated, and is based on the increasing definition of location and origin, along with regulations about grape yield, grape type, alcoholic strength etc. The top classification is AOC – *Appellation d'Origine Contrôlée*, which appears as, say, Appellation Bordeaux Contrôlée on the label itself. Next is VDQS, *Vin Délimité de Qualité Supérieure*, which are wines that are not quite AOC, and after that is *Vin de Pays*, 'country wine', which can be very good value.

Alsace
In many respects, Alsace has the best of two worlds; it produces French-style dry wine from German grape varieties, and produces them at a price that many people in the trade consider to be cheap. Alsace seems to make many people's third or fourth favourite wine.

Throughout much of its history Alsace has been a contested border area; sometimes French and sometimes German. Alsace wines have their own classification system alongside the national one. This is similar in style to the German one, but quite unlike it, works very well. The lowest is Edelzwicker, not for ageing, then on progressively to Alsace AC, Alsace Grand Cru, Vendange tardive, to Sélection de grains nobles. Alsatian regulations are very strictly enforced, and there has never been any funny business in this region; the art of serious, honest wine-making prospers here as in few other places.

Alsatian wines age very well, and as more people discover that they are excellent value for money, so the overall price seems destined to rise. One investment ploy may be to buy wines from those vineyards which are seeking classification as Grands Crus and which will be able to charge more once they do.

Grape varieties are the most prominent feature on an Alsatian wine label. The main varieties are Riesling, Gewürztraminer and Tokay Pinot Gris.

Good vintages: '88, '87, '86, '85+, '84, '83+, '82, '78, '76.
(+ after year means excellent)

Some of the best producers:
Léon Beyer
Blanck
Dopff au Moulin
Dopff et Irion
Théo Faller
Rolly Gassmann
Hugel et Fils
Kientzler
Domaine Klipfel
Marc Kreydenweiss
Kuentz-Bas
Jos Meyer
A & O Muré
Jean Preiss-Zimmer
Pierre Sparr
F. E. Trimbach
Zind-Humbrecht.

Bordeaux

No one needs telling that some of the finest wines in the world come from Bordeaux; nor that they command some of the highest prices. Anyone who can afford Latour, Lafite and Pétrus should buy them and drink them with pleasure. But most of us can't, and perhaps, relatively fewer and fewer of us will be able to. Bordeaux nevertheless produces a huge amount of quality wine that can usefully be investigated by anyone who likes this style of wine.

The cheapest way to enjoy the fine wines is to buy the cheaper 'bad' years, and 'second' wines. 'Bad' years usually mean bad for investment. These are not years when the wine is undrinkable, but rather that it is not going to live for twenty years in the bottle. Most are drinkably mature sooner than that, and can be cheap. Second wines are produced by some of the great châteaux, and tend to be surplus wine, young vine crop, or barrels that didn't quite meet their high standards. They are widely available now, and in fact Marks & Spencer, among others, stock a large range of them.

The system of classification which produced what are called classed growths was established in the Médoc in 1855, and ranked the châteaux into five classes and the Cru Bourgeois, according to the prices those wines were making then. Some things have changed a lot since 1855, but in fact the order of châteaux has not changed significantly. Only one château has managed to change class, Mouton-Rothschild going up to a first growth after fifty years of campaigning.

Today there are the 'super seconds' and others which outperform their class, and the prices these wines fetch is very high, although lower than if they were to be reclassified. However many personal re-classifications are attempted by writers and others in the trade, no final word on the subject is possible. The benefit for us is that as higher prices are concentrated in the classed growths, so the prices of other wines outside that system are relatively better value. The words, 'Grand Vin' on a bottle, however, means nothing other than that the owner thinks it is.

Bordeaux is one of the largest wine-producing regions in the world, with many thousands of properties, of which many hundreds produce high-quality wines at good value prices. The area itself is not the most scenic, but for the wine-lover there are few opportunities to visit as many interesting vineyards in one area as there are here. Getting round 4,000 vineyards in a three-week holiday is not possible, so if you want to visit a few the best way is to chat up your local quality wine-merchant and use their networks to arrange visits; most will be happy to do it, especially if you are a regular customer. The merchant, if he or she is any good, will have visited the region, and will have discovered good-value châteaux, but thankfully for us, the real costs of these visits are not borne by the price of those wines, but rather by the higher-priced châteaux, whose names can better accommodate the addition of these costs. So the net result is that these petits châteaux reach us in a subsidized form.

Sweet wines are a difficult area and a specialized one. Most people love them or hate them. I love them. The finest come from Sauternes and Barsac, which also were given a classification in 1855, into one Grand Premier Cru – Ch. d'Yquem, ten Premiers Crus, and twelve existing Deuxièmes Crus. Other sweet wines come from Cadillac and Ste-Croix-du-Mont, and are much cheaper. 1986 and 1988 were exceptional years in Sauternes, and if you like this style of wine both should be large buys.

The key to value in Bordeaux is to reach out from the centre, the

Haut-Médoc, into the more outlying areas, where the good value is. Across the river lies one area that could no longer be described as underpriced, Pomerol. This region was 'promoted' by the leading wine-dealer and merchant in the area, Jean-Pierre Moueix. The most expensive claret, Ch. Pétrus, comes from here, and many other properties have risen on its coat-tails. They are certainly good wines, but they are certainly not cheap. Whether Fronsac and Canon-Fronsac, neighbouring sites where 'Pomerolization' is occurring, will rise to similar but lesser prominence is generally debated in the trade.

One of the questions we would all like the answer to is how to buy good Bordeaux cheaply. Yes, of course, wine-merchants have to make a living, but how can we best find good value? I suppose the question comes down to 'what do wine merchants themselves drink, and where do they buy it from?' I asked one, John Wilson of Buckingham Fine Wines, to list his 'undervalued properties':

Classed growths
Ch. La Lagune
Ch. Branaire-Ducru
Ch. Talbot
Ch. Gruaud-Larose
Ch. Giscours
Ch. Prieuré-Lichine

Cru Bourgeois
Ch. Potensac
Ch. d'Angludet
Ch. Chasse-Spleen
Ch. Haut-Marbuzet
Ch. de Pez
Ch. Meyney
Ch. Sociando-Mallet
Ch. du Tertre
Ch. Larmande
Ch. La Dominique
Ch. de Sales
Clos du Clocher
Ch. Clos René
Clos des Jacobins
Ch. Fourcas-Hosten
Ch. Brillette

Fronsac/Canon-Fronsac
Ch. Canon
Ch. la Rivière

Sauternes
Ch. Bastor-Lamontagne
Ch. Doisy-Daëne
Ch. Nairac

Second wines
Clos du Marquis
Les Forts de Latour
Haut-Bages-Averous
Lacoste-Borie

He adds two good buys from the southern Rhône, Châteauneuf-du-Pape – Ch. Beaucastel and Domaine du Vieux Télégraphe.

Few, if any of these wines should be above £15, and many under £10, especially if bought from one of the merchants below. There is often no strict wholesale/retail division in the wine trade because the product is not amenable to that, but there are some merchants' lists which are watched more closely than others by members of the trade, both because they are cheap, and because they have a very fast turnover of quality wines. These are the lists John follows most closely, and which he will buy from, sometimes to re-sell within the trade (at a higher price, of course).

Nigel Baring, 20d Ranston St, London NW1 6SY (071-724 0836)
[Buckingham Trading Co., 68 Alpha St, Slough, Berks SL1 1QX (0753-21336)]
College Cellar/La Réserve (not cheap), 56 Walton St, London, SW3 1RB (071-589 2020)
Corney & Barrow (Mark Bedini, on the wholesale side), 12 Helmet Row, London, EC1V 3QJ (071-251 4051)
Farr Vintners (one of the best), 19 Sussex St, London SW1V 4RR (071-828 1960)
R. C. Gold, Park House, Church Rd, Saffron Walden, Essex (0799-40699)
Ernst Gorge, 245 Whitechapel Rd, London E1 1DB (071-247 1324)
Richard Kihl, 164 Regent's Park Rd, London NW3 8XN (071-586 5911)
Kurtz & Chan Wines, 1 Duke of York St, London SW1 6JP (071-930 6981)

Champagne

Almost all the Champagne sold is far too young to drink; that shouldn't surprise us, given what we know about the wine industry, but sadly, most people buy a bottle to celebrate a specific event, and tend to buy and consume immediately. This is definitely not the way to enjoy this wine.

Generally what has happened to the market is that the Champenois have become used to asking for more money for their product, while the supermarkets have driven the price in the shop down, leaving us, the buyers, with a product that has barely left childhood, let alone started on puberty. Some very acidic vintages are now being used in the blends, and high *dosage*, the addition of cane sugar to sweeten the wine, is now very noticeable. High acidity is not a problem for us, as we shall be keeping the wine for a while anyway, but high *dosage* is bad, as maturation will not bring these wines round, they will only fall apart. At a recent tasting of twenty-five Champagnes available from high-street shops, I found only six that would repay keeping:

Safeway, Albert Etienne
Tesco
Majestic, J. de Telmont
Co-op (CWS), Champagne de Clairveaux
Marks & Spencer, NV, Desroches & Cie
Eldridge Pope, Chairman's Dry.

The river Saône 1. Burgundy: the golden slope

Likely to be a short section in a book about reasonably priced wines. Many people believe that the wines of Burgundy are overpriced; others think quite the opposite; however, most agree that Chablis is expensive, to the point when even an expensive restaurant like Le Gavroche in London can add a note to their wine list to the effect that they consider these wines too poor value for money to list extensively.

There are some wines from this region which are still excellent value for money. Dream about Romanée-Conti, Vougeot, and Montrachet, but buy:

Côte de Nuits: Fixin, Marsannay.
Côte de Beaune: Auxey-Duresses, Chorey-lès-Beaune, Savigny-lès-Beaune, Monthélie, Santenay, St-Aubin (red and white), St-Romain (white).
Côte Chalonnaise is generally very good value: Mercurey, Givry, Montagny.
The Mâconnais: St-Véran, Pouilly-Vinzelles, Mâcon-Viré, Mâcon-Clessé, Mâcon-Lugny.

None of these are long-term keeping wines, but all will develop well over a period of about five years.

The main problem about Burgundy is in knowing the good producers and *negociants*, and to some extent knowing who's on the way up or down. It's here that the small-scale, specialized wine merchant really earns his keep, by developing a thorough knowledge of the area. This is the only way to find good value Burgundy, so pick your merchant.

A few words about the beauty of wonderful Burgundy: it is one of the few wines that makes converts, and about which people have passionate disputes. When it is good it has a perfume that is unmatchable, and on the palate a sophistication and fleetingness that is both beautiful and sad. Overblown words for an underappreciated wine; it's easy to feel that way about this subject.

The river Saône 2. Beaujolais

Not a name that some would associate with maturing wine, corrupted, as the name is, by the immediate association with Nouveau. Beaujolais Nouveau is a waste of most people's time and money, unlike matured Beaujolais, which can taste like Burgundy. That is strange, given that the grape varieties are quite different, the Gamay being grown in Beaujolais, the Pinot Noir north in Burgundy.

There are now 10 Beaujolais Crus, or top growing areas, although the most recent member, Regnié, has yet to make many people believe that it is worthy of the elevation. The crus in general worth keeping to mature are:
Côte de Brouilly
Juliénas
Morgon (especially Burgundy-like)
Moulin-à-Vent.

Rhône, north

A few years ago the Rhône would have been many people's favourite area for good-value wines, but not any more. Those wines which have escalated in price very much are: Condrieu, Cornas, Côte Rôtie, Hermitage and Ch. Grillet. Better value can be found among Crozes-Hermitage, both white and red, and St-Joseph, which is more generally available but shorter lived.

Rhône, south

Châteauneuf-du-Pape is generally undervalued, perhaps partly because it is considered to be unfashionable. Other areas where good value, but generally a lower level of quality is reached are:
Côtes du Lubéron
Côtes du Rhône-Villages
Lirac
Gigondas

There is a flavour, rich, sometimes creamy, sturdy and with a particular length of fruit, that Rhône wines offer, and that their fans look for. Once hooked, there's no going back.

The Loire

Six hundred miles is a long way for a river to travel, and it's particularly hard to follow it when so many wonderful wines are made along its banks.

Sancerre and Pouilly Fumé

Grown across the river from each other, the Pouilly Fumé is fuller, sturdier wine than Sancerre, which is sharp, zingy, fruity, and bone dry. Both are made from the Sauvignon Blanc grape, and both can develop in the bottle for a very long time – twenty years is not inconceivable. It's very hard to buy aged Sauvignon, so to experience that taste at all it might be necessary to keep the bottle yourself. Neighbouring Reuilly, Quincy, and Ménétou-Salon are not so adaptable to ageing, but worth a couple of years of anyone's time.

Vouvray and Montlouis

Also across the river from each other, and both made from the Chenin Blanc grape. They are also made in dry, sweet, and sparkling versions. The Chenin Blanc grape has been recently 'discovered' in California, where they are making some fashionable wines from it. As a source of light, fruity, refreshing wine, the Chenin may have nowhere to go but up and the same is true of the quality wines made from the grape. Sparkling Vouvray, Pétillant or Mousseux can last for 10 years or longer. Sweet Vouvray Moelleux can also last as long.

Savennières

Another Chenin product, and a very small AC. The wines are among the longest lived along the Loire, and really start from four years and go on as long as twenty. Sadly, Savennières has become better known recently, and prices have gone up. Two of the best are: Coulée de Serrant and Roche aux Moines.

Muscadet

Yes, you can mature Muscadet, although certainly most will not improve, as they're made to be drunk young. The bottle must say 'Muscadet Sevre et Maine', which is the best part of the region, and *'sur lie'* – i.e. it was rested on its lees (grape debris and dead yeast cells). This gives it greater lasting power, and the flavour of a real wine that needn't be chilled to zero. New regulations are favoured by some Muscadet makers to get the message about different quality levels across better, as top-quality Muscadets can last twenty years or even more.

Sweet Loire

Some sweet wines of really superb quality are made on the Loire:
    Coteaux de l'Aubance
    Coteaux du Layon

Bonnezeauz
Quarts de Chaume.
Ten years is only the start of the lives of these wines, but the bad thing is their immediate accessibility; they tend to get drunk too soon. The unpopularity of sweet wines generally, and ones from the Loire in particular, is demonstrated by the fact that Coteaux du Layon land is the cheapest AOC land in France, which is good news for those who like these wines. Buy only in good years: '88, '85, '83, '78.

Red Loire
Red Sancerres, made from Pinot Noir, age but are rather expensive, Chinon and Bourgueil will certainly age, and are mainly made from the Cabernet Franc, and there is also red Anjou, a more interesting wine than the white, and certainly the pink Anjou.

These wines have a particular character which many people love, and others hate. My own feeling is against them, as I don't like their effusiveness, nor the hard stalky flavour. They can be very long lived.

The South
Some very good wines indeed are being made in the warmth of the south of France. Here are the results of two tasting sessions, one in London and one conducted in the region. Please see page 95 for the key to the tasting system employed in this book.

Minervois
*Ch. de Paraza, 1988, 2–4+ years. Very young now, deep ruby, lots of full fruit on nose. Very tannic, quite rich and balanced fruit; rich, elegant, and nice acidity. Robert Parker has already been here, sadly, so the price can only go one way. Buy a lot; their representatives for the UK are Mistral Wines (for address see page 135). (Oddbins currently stock it.)

Tour St Martin, 1987, 2–4 years. Good nose, nice fruit and tannin, quite full, good structure, fruit will come through nicely.

Ch. la Voulte Gasparets, 1986, 1–3 years. Nice, complex nose, nice fruit, very dry, lots of acidity and tannin; better on nose than palate.

– 1985, 1 year. Good berry fruit on nose, vegetal and ripe. Very powerful, lots of tannin, but fruit is not dense enough to live much longer.

Domaine de Villemajou, 1979, 1–2 years. Startlingly good wine, full, flowery tar on nose. Nice structure, still quite tannic, complex, and very mature fruit. Actually almost fully mature.

Corbières
Ch. de Lastours, Cuvée Simon Descamps, 1988, 2–4 years. A very full, rich wine, excellent pre-balance, supple, soft tannin, good rich fruit.

– 1986. Even better.

By way of novelty: Paul Herpé et Fils (Rue de la Tonnellerie, 11104 Narbonne, France, Tel: 68 32 03 25) will sell you wine in a barrel. When people regularly used to buy by the cask they used to get together and have bottling parties, which must have been fun. This is one of the few companies to continue with the tradition of selling in the wood.

The company started in 1919 as a mail-order wine merchant, when it was not standard to sell wine from the winery by the bottle. They still have 7,000 customers in France, but the complications of sending the wine to the UK means that it's unlikely to catch on here. They send wine in four sizes of barrel, which is made out of chestnut and carries a FF30 deposit. Paul Herpé's best wine is Château de Réveillon 1987, if you want to order some.

Fitou
Cooperative Tuchan, 1988, 2–3 years. Good character of fruit, lots of tannin, good potentially light wine.

Cooperative Villeneuve, 1988, 2–4+ years. Very young, good fruit, good soft tannin on finish, excellent potential.

Ch. La Grange, 1988 (red), 2–5 years. Very full fruit on nose, jammy, big tannic finish. Lot of slightly flabby fruit, astringent finish, stalky, fiery; not a choice drinking wine now, but will develop into a very decent wine for the price.

Sadly under-represented in the UK are the wines of the **St Chinian** in the Languedoc. They keep and are very cheap at the moment. St Chinian is one of my tips for a wine with a future, and holiday buying there is a good idea.

Côtes du Roussillon–Villages, which incorporates the very high quality region of Collioure; it's patchy but is an area to watch as some enterprising wine-makers are starting to produce good wines there.

Cahors can be very long-lived, but some people question whether the wait is worth it. Well, sometimes yes, especially wines from those companies which have started to make more modern styles of wine.

Jurançon Moelleux, a stunning sweet wine, very, very long lived, quite expensive, and hard to find except in the quality merchants.

Monbazillac, also sweet, cheaper, and very long lived.

Madiran, produces some very good value wines, and one appears in the next chapter, from Sainsbury's.

Pacherenc du Vic-Bilh, very fine wines, almost impossible to find in the UK.

Banyuls, fortified and will live forever, almost. Lighter than Port, it has a woody flavour, and sometimes is described in French as being *'rancio'*, which means not putrid but leathery or walnutty in a high way. **Rancio** is a recurrent theme and flavour in this part of the world, and Sherry may be its highest expression.

Alps: Savoie produces some interesting wines, one from the Mondeuse grape produces powerful reds near Chambéry; the Jacquère white grape near Apremert (Tesco's is a good example), and others. Jura is famous for Vin Jaune, made from Savagnin grapes which have been hung and dried, and tastes like a Sherry, and will live a long time in the bottle. The best is AC Château Chalon.

Italy

Italy has everything the Good Cellar person might be looking for; new wines which rise in price, experiments with grape varieties and technology and a difficult system of regulation which doesn't really work, but can offer the enthusiast hours of administrative 'pleasure'.

Italy also produces more wine lake trash than any other country, and but for the fact that some of the wines of France need to be illegally beefed up by Italian wines, and but for the German wine industry's need for a cheap wine base, a lot of very bad wine-makers would go out of business. Good riddance. Some notorious Italian 'wine-makers' have killed people with chemical brews that were unfit for human consumption, and designed only to get a subsidy from the EC.

Italy has three wine quality levels, starting with DOCG, *Denominazione di Orgine Controllata e Garantita*, followed by DOC (minus the *Garantita*) and lastly *Vino da tavola*. Some of the finest wines in Italy are actually *Vini da tavola*, because they have been made from grape varieties that are outside the local regulations, such as Cabernet Sauvignon, and some of these are called 'super Tuscans', for obvious reasons. Strangely, it is the local aristocrats, some of whom have made wine for over 500 years, who have led this revolution in wine-making practices.

Some of these wines are hugely expensive and represent little or no value for money, but the second division of these are very classy wines indeed, and are good value for money. Among the great names of Italy – Barolo, Barbaresco and Brunello di Montalcino – change is taking place more slowly, if at all. These wines are not bad value in world terms, if you like the herby quality that so many Italian wines seem to possess.

Piedmont, in the north of Italy, is the home of Barolo and Barbaresco. Barolo is the archetypal big, full-bodied red wine, ideal with heavy food. Currently there is a dispute between the traditionalists and the modernists; the latter want to make a fruity, more accessible wine, and the traditionalists want to leave the wine in oak for years. The modernists have an eye on the export trade, something the traditionalists have never found easy.

Lombardy is a bit of a desert for fine wines, with certain notable exceptions, one of whom is Maurizio Zanella of Ca' del Bosco. His sparkling wine is the most widely available, but all his wines are rather expensive. Lugana can age for a while, and is a nice example of a full-bodied, fruity white wine.

Alto Adige (Südtirol) produces some interesting wines, red and white, especially from J. Hofstätter. The Veneto is super *vino da tavola* country. The wine PR machine has yet to take up this area fully, but it can't be long as some of the wines from here are underpriced. I like chilled Valpolicella, even on a hot day in London, but it's not for laying down, although a super-Valpolicella, Recioto, can be; both dry (*amarone*), and sweet (*amabile*). Both wines are made from partly dried grapes.

Companies such as Masi, Anselmi, Pieropan (Soave) and Tedeschi are good, but the best, arguably, is Venegazzù-Conte Loredan-Gasparini, two of whose wines, della Casa and Etichetta Nera, are huge complex wines of the highest quality and very good value.

Tuscany is the centre of the Italian wine world. Sassicaia, made from 100% Cabernet Sauvignon and the first of the Super Tuscans was made here, and a growing circle of wine-makers has followed the lead.

Traditionally the home of the DOCG Chianti, and also of Italy's most expensive wine, Biondi-Santi's Brunello di Montalcino. This wine can mature over huge lengths of time, and sell for huge amounts of money. In 1991 the Masters of Wine will visit Tuscany and (briefly) Umbria, in one of those mass visits that did so much to put Australia and Chile on the world wine map. Similar high street penetration should be expected from this trip. See page 71 for a tasting of Tuscan '85 wines.

Umbria is a land of few stars but a few bright lights: Lungarotti produces some fine wines, such as Rubesco di Torgiano, and Antinori, one of the best Tuscan names, also makes wine here.

The South. Not a source of much that is worth knowing about, but there are a few that merit our interest. In Campania there are wines made by Mastroberardino, widely available but a little expensive. The Basilicata region, roughly the instep of Italy's foot, has one wine which is very good indeed: Aglianico del Vulture, made from the Aglianico grape. Fratelli d'Angelo make the best.

The Apulia region is the home of the Torre company which produces a range of wines, among them Torre Ercolana, especially 1979. Michael Broadbent wrote about it rather famously in *Decanter*: 'I am a claret man . . . I did not like [it]. Strawberry red; pig sty smell and taste (butyric acid?), highish volatile acidity and a hot, raw, sharp finish. £8.95! Give me a modestly priced Spanish or Portuguese wine any day.' Personally, I quite like it.

I visited and interviewed a wine-seller in Milan with over 40 years experience, to ask his advice on Italian wines worth keeping. Fausto Provera's long established shop (7 Corso Magenta) may sadly have already been sold, as none of Mr Provera's three sons is interested in following him into the wine trade.

Some wines to keep
Inferno
Sassella
Sforzato di Spina
Amarone Valpolicella (Recioto)

He is very concerned about the effects of light on wine, especially on white wine, which will maderize them (make them taste of Madeira when they shouldn't). He finds that he comes across this quite frequently, but thinks that this happens because wine is too often on display in Italy.

Some cheaper wines
Pomino Beneficio
Pomino Bianco
Vernaccia di San Gimignano
Greco di Tufo
Lacryma Christi
Verduzzo demi-sec
Sauvignon
Pinot Grigio
Pinot Bianco

Much more expensive is Picolit, a sweet wine once known as the 'Yquem of Italy'; many of the vineyards have been damaged although there is still some production.

Cheaper wines from Alto Adige, white
Gewürztraminer
Riesling Renano
Weissburgunder
Kerner
Red
Lago di Caldaro
Lagrein Dunkel
Blauburgunder
Cabernet Sauvignon

Signor Provera is not sure Biondi-Santi's Brunello is worth the money, but he certainly likes it. He recommends '82, '83 and '85 as good years. The oldest bottle he has on sale is Biondi-Santi 1888, which in the summer of 1989 was priced at 15 million lire (£8,000). A little more accessible is one from 1951, a favourite vintage of his, at 650,000 lire (£300).

A few years ago he had problems when he had to move out of the cellars he had always used, originally a Roman prison. Moving to smaller premises, he found he had to slim down the stock somewhat, as he had acquired the massive quantity of 180,000 bottles.

Tuscany 1985 – buy, buy and buy again
1985 was a great vintage in Tuscany, considered the best since 1971, and the first good one under DOCG regulations. Below is the result of a tasting of these wines at, and mostly available from, Winecellars in London: 153/5 Wandsworth High Street, London SW18 4JB (Tel: 081-871 2668). The most recent word is that 1988 will also be an excellent vintage, so buy nothing serious until these wines are released, unless it is more '85s.

Chianto Classico region

Cepparello, Isole e Olena, 1985 (£10.00), 3–5 years. Deep ruby, intense spice and tar on the nose. Concentrated good fruit, long very hard tannic finish, rich and good weight.

Chianti Classico Riserva, Felsina Berardenga, 1985 (£7.00), 2–4 years. Jammy, plummy fruit on nose, lots of tannin, some acidity, full, harsh finish.

√ Fontalloro, Felsina Berardenga, 1985 (£11.00), 3–5 years. A superb wine; deep ruby colour, lovely spicy fruit on nose, elegant balanced tight fruit, ripe and peachy; good full soft tannin. Excellent.

√ Chianti Classico Riserva, Castello di Cacchiano, 1985 (£7.00), 2–3 years. Light ruby; elegant, possibly thin fruit on nose, nice tannic finish, some elegance and subtlety; an almost Burgundian lingering on the palate.

*Chianti Classico Riserva, 'Millennio', Castello di Cacchiano, 1985 (£10.00), 3–5+ years. Very elegant ruby, rather closed nose, full and rich fruit, excellent length, complex and classy.

√ Chianti Classico Riserva, Fontodi, 1985 (£8.50), 2–4 years. Full nose, meaty, very young colour. Big tannic finish, rich fruit, full, a nice wine.

√ Chianti Classico Riserva, Riecine, 1985 (£14.00) 4–6 years. Lovely damson, spicy fruit on nose, massive tannin, big and dense, very big and raw, with all the ingredients to become a wonderful wine.

√ Chianti Classico La Gioia, Riecine, 1985 (£16.75), 3–6 years. Balanced fruit, stalky, tarry spice on nose; great ageing potential, very classy and balanced.

Vino da Tavola, Sammarco, Castello dei Rampolla, 1985 (£20.00), 3–7 years. Very intense colour; luscious nose, herbal and spicy, currently short on palate; some classy, elegant fruit, hot, full and rich. This wine may develop into a bottle worth spending £20 for, or it may not.

√ Chianti Classico Riserva, Castello di Volpaia, 1985 (£7.00), 2–5 years. Ruby, garnet rim; shy and perfumed, tobacco nose. Lean, hard concentrated tannic nose, light fruit, almost grapey, good structure and quite classy.

The next region, **Chianti Rufina** is less fashionable, and therefore cheaper.

Chianti Rufina Riserva, Selvapiano, 1985 (£5.00), 2–4 years. Fleshy, alcoholic nose; thin fruit, some light tannin, not much depth. This may come right, but it's not the bargain it is claimed to be.

*Chianti Rufina Riserva Villa di Ventrice, 1985 (£4.50) 3–5+ years. Fantastic value, and a definite buy. Excellent concentrated fruit on nose, huge tannins, with a lovely depth of fruit. There are few better value wines than this around.

Carmigano; even cheaper

*√ Carmigano Riserva, Villa di Capezzana, 1985 (£9.00), 2–4 years.

Lean, savoury damson nose; complex and reserved, good rich fruit, mellow tannins, long and firm, excellent fruit on finish.

**Ghiaie della Furba, Villa di Capezzana, 1985 (£9.00), 2–4 years. A fabulous, luscious wine. Bordeaux grape varieties, herby, cedary nose, lovely balance; rich, complex fruit, light tannins. Wonderful combination of fruit and complexity. A definite buy.

Spain

Spanish wine used to be synonymous with the worst kind of hang-overs and a waste of time and money. There was a lot of that, and there is still, but there are also some bright spots. Rioja is not what it was. This used to be one of the few regions that kept wine until it was ready, but today the wines are not always made to last, or are being released too early. Other regions such as Penedès, Navarra, Ribera del Duero and Toro are making wines that are as fine as any of their quality status in the world.

Rioja *bodegas*, or wineries, which still make good wine, and which are concentrating their production on *crianza* (oak-aged) wines, instead of *sin crianza* are:
  La Rioja Alta
  Bilainas
  Campo Viejo
  CVNE
  Muga
  Marqués de Murrieta

Catalonia and Penedès
There has been a wine-making revolution here. There are three companies of interest: Jean León, Raimat and Torres.

Jean León, who now lives in California, was the first to plant Cabernet Sauvignon in Catalonia and his company has stayed a small, high-quality producer. At the moment the mixture is of Cabernet Sauvignon and Franc but they are growing Merlot and this will be included soon (if it is not secretly so already). The 1981 is wonderfully mature but should keep for two years at this level – lovely nutty nose, mature cedary sweetness, elegant, tarry fruit, long and complex. The '83 is not quite so good – full ripe fruit on nose, lots of depth, very dry on the finish, hard and austere, but the weight of fruit is a little light; one to four years. The 1987 Chardonnay is a superb wine – buttery fruit on the nose, rich and clean, very full. A lot of unknit American oak flavours on the palate at the moment, ripe, tight fruit, and in one to three years will be good 'austere' style Chardonnay.

Torres is one of the most famous wine names in the world, and many of their wines are of top quality, especially the Gran Coronas, and Coronas Black Label. Few if any wine producers can match the range of wine they produce either in range or in depth of quality. Worth keeping are Milmanda Chardonnay and the two Coronas wines. Other producers to look out for are Masía Bach, René Barbier and Can Ràfols des Caus. In Navarra there is one estate that produces high quality wines, Señorio de Sarria.

Ribera del Duero

Vega Silicia, Spain's greatest wine is made in this region. It is very, very expensive and rare, and the vineyard is famous for being probably the most remote in the world, an eyrie high in the Duero valley. The wine is not offered for sale until it is sixteen years old; it is not made in bad years, and takes twenty to thirty years to reach its peak.

This region as a whole is likely to become the premier region of wine in Spain. The next greatest wine made in the region is Pesquera, which Robert Parker calls the Pétrus of Spain, and prices have risen sharply, although a recent vintage can still be bought for under £40, a lot cheaper than Ch. Pétrus. This wine may be worth buying into for investment reasons. Also try Bodegas Mauro and Ribera del Duero Coop.

The best value of all in this area is to be found in Toro, where two producers make very alcoholic wine (14 per cent): Bodegas Farina and Bodegas Louis Mateos. There are, I believe, few wines of better value in the world than these. Not a small claim. The Farina Gran Colegiata, '85 and '86 are excellent wines. The '86 is an exceptional wine, and over the next two to three years or so will open and develop into a very good quality wine. Buy now.

Sherry is not usually thought of as a wine to lay down, because it does not develop in the bottle, and we usually buy it in the bottle. It starts off in a wooden cask, of course. In fact, in Jerez, it is possible to make an investment in *en primeur* Sherry in the cask. The small producers who make the high-quality Almacenista Sherries, sell the casks to *Almacenistas*, amateurs, who hold the wine and free the capital of the companies for other things. Subsequently, the companies buy it back from the groups of amateurs at a profit for the investors. Anyone who goes to Spain a lot, or who has a house there, could get involved with this: enquire at Lustau in Jerez, or at some of the smaller producers direct.

Some will blanche, but personally I love the flavour of *fino* Sherry that has been kept for a few years, the bottle upright, and then chilled. It doesn't have the light freshness usually associated with *fino*, the lightest and driest Sherry style. Try Berry Bros own label.

Portugal

One of those moments, later seen to be significant, happened to me in Portugal. We went to dinner at a lovely restuarant, the Poa de Trigo at Cabo de Roca, just outside Lisbon, and the wine list was a revelation. It listed wines, some over twenty years old, for a fraction of the price that similarly long-lived wines from France or even Spain would have cost. We had a couple of bottles, and they were lovely. I had found that, even as a poor student, I could afford to drink mature fine wines, and I suppose the gestation of this book had begun.

For our purposes, Portugal's classification system is user-friendly, because it divides all its wine into either Vinhos Verdes, literally, green or young wines, and Vinhos Maduros, wine that can be or has been aged. Some producers still have the good habit of keeping their wine until they are mature.

In terms of the overall industry, Portugal has some of the best and worst of the modern and old world. Too many producers are happy to produce the heavy, oxidized monsters that Spain used to make so much of, but, happily, there are also very go-ahead firms for whom the future seems to be rosy. Barca Velha, Portugal's equivalent to Spain's Vega Sicilia, is also made in the Douro river valley, by Ferreira.

Small areas worth exploring are Bucelas, Carcavelhos, now almost built over, and Colares, where the vines grow in the sand at the beach. Larger areas are Dão, and Bairrada. Garrafeiras are merchants' premium wines, sometimes blends, and are excellent value for laying down. I have some 1975 Casaleiro Garrafeiras doing very well indeed (wardrobe bottom). The company J. M. da Fonseca (not related to the Port company) produce wines with a future, and a more expensive but hugely long-lived wine, red and white, comes from Buçaco. Cornering the 1944 white Buçaco, or a Colares vintage is a possibility for the mini-plutocrat.

And then there is Port. There are a number of views as to whether investing in Port is a good idea. Essentially it depends on what you think will happen in the future, and then betting on it. Port has been bought by the Americans, and so it has had a certain fashion, but I wonder whether it will last. The only real indicator to future price is future demand, and this is where the theories about Port get tied up. No one thinks there will be problem with future demand for Bordeaux, but Port is different.

Another idea is to look at Madeira. Madeira has been out of fashion for a long time. If you've never tried it, and think that sweet Sherry is cloying, but like the consistency and would prefer a bit more bite and some acidity, then think about Madeira. Madeira is cooked at 40°C and is one of the toughest and longest-lived wines in the world. There are four grades, in ascending sweetness: Sercial (dry), Verdelho, Bual, Malmsey. The last two are the highest qualities. Buying vintage Madeira is really something your parents ought to have done, as it takes fifty years to get near its best, but it has other qualities that make it accessible earlier, and therefore cheaper. For the investor, I think Madeira might be worth a small punt. But a very small one. If you like this style of wine, then Moscatel de Setúbal is a cheaper alternative, and very pleasant.

Germany

The surprising thing about German wines is not the huge gulf in quality between the most horrible Liebfraumilch, and a stunning, elegant 1976 Riesling Auslese, but that both sides in this quality divide should be organized by strict regulation, to no effect at all.

The key to the problem is crop yield. The German system for classifying quality is based on the ripeness of the grapes, and thus on sugar content. However, there are no regulations as to the yield of grapes from a vine, so improving the eventual quality of the wine by pruning back only happens at the best estates. Most tragic of all, the names of these great and good estates are often not dissimilar to the ones which practice much lower forms of quality control.

The finest German wines are not cheap, but just below this top level prices are very reasonable, especially compared to France. The world does not trade in German wines, so only the very top ones are sold at premium prices. There are two levels of quality, one abbreviated to QbA, and the one we are interested in, QmP – Qualitätswein mit Prädikat, within which level there are six divisions of increasing quality: Kabinett, Spätlese, Auslese, Beerenauslese, Trockenbeerenauslese, Eiswein (made from frozen grapes).

Then the regional names take over. The river Mosel is at the centre of quality German wine-making, and the Riesling grape is the source of the finest wines of all. It is hard to justify spending the money to buy these wines to keep, when they are cheaply available now in a fully mature state at auctions. Of course, this will not continue for much longer, for reasons of diminishing supply, history and currency. It will become sensible to start storing these wines if the Germans start drinking a lot more themselves or if other people do, like the East Germans, or the Japanese. The Sanyo company has just bought part of the von Buhl estate, one of the best run in Germany. Clearly Sanyo thinks there is a big market for German wines in Japan, which would make sense, as it goes well with their food. If the Japanese start to develop a taste for fine German wines, then, of course, there is no ceiling to prices. My advice is to get in on the ground floor. Some of the top names are: J. J. Prüm; Egon Müller; von Hövel; Dr Fischer; Zilliken; von Schubert; F. W. Gymnasium; F. Haag.

Austria

The year 1984 was not good for the Austrian wine industry. The diethylene glycol scandal meant that exports of wine fell from 490,000 hectolitres, to 42,000, in 1986. That low figure may be improving, but perhaps not by much. What the scandal started, the new wine laws have compounded. Intended to be the strictest in the world, they are also a huge barrier for a small quality producer to leap over. For Austrian wine to be taken seriously again, the quality wine must lead the way, making it desired as a product.

But, for us, the greater the difficulty, the greater the possible advantage. If you go rooting around in Austria you will come upon wonderful little wine-makers whose wine is impossible to buy in the UK. It's worth doing. They have an indigenous grape variety called the Grüner Veltliner, which produces dry, peppery white wine that is very good, and some of the sweet wines are superb. If it were possible to find some of these wines in the UK, I would recommend buying. Sadly, they are not. Still, there's nowhere to go but up.

Bulgaria

The Bulgarians effectively subsidize their wine exports, which means that we are getting very good value for money; Bulgarian Cabernet Sauvignon is now the best selling red wine in the UK.

They have developed their own version of the French regulatory system, the top one being Controliran, and next Reserve, and these wines tend to be sold when mature or very nearly so. None are long-term laying down wines, but some will repay a few years, and they will certainly form the backbone of many day-to-day drinking cellars. I asked Don Philpot who wrote *The Wine and Food of Bulgaria* (Mitchell Beazley, 1989), for his top ten Bulgarian wines to lay down. Few shops hold the full range, but most will stock a few; all are under £5.

1. Cabernet Sauvignon, 1985, Suhindol. Made in the northern region, near the Danube. Big bodied, dry, aged in oak casks for 3 years; deep ruby, powerful blackcurrant nose, nice tannin.

2. Oriachovitza Reserve Cabernet Sauvignon, 1983. Oriachovitza is the hilly part of southern Bulgaria. Lots of blackcurrant fruit, stylish, mature fruit, good balance.

3. Damianitza Reserve Melnik, 1983. Made from an indigenous grape variety, the Melnik, produced in the south west, near Greece. Full and dry, lots of fruit and oak, and can be compared with a Burgundy or a Châteauneuf-du-Pape.

4. Stambolovo Merlot, 1983. Fragrant, fruity nose, light and mellow, will age very well.

5. Assenovgrad Mavrud, 1981. Another indigenous grape variety, the Mavrud, produced in the Rhodope mountains, near the Turkish border. Good depth of colour, intense bouquet, minty, full bodied, good firm tannin still.

6. Sakar Mountain Cabernet, 1983. Produced in the south, intensely blackcurranty, dry, full bodied and great depth.

7. Svischtov Cabernet Sauvignon, 1985. Produced in the north from vineyards overlooking the Danube. Elegant, tawny colour, rich and intense fruit and oak.

8. Oriachovita Cabernet Sauvignon/Merlot, 1983. A particularly good region for red wines; concentrated mature fruit, farmyardy, rich and soft.

9. Sunhindol Gamza, 1984. Made from a native grape variety, fresh, clean and fruity, will develop complexity.

10. Assenovgrad Mavrud, 1984. Big and full bodied, great depth of colour, dry, plummy, and aromatic and minty.

Yugoslavia

In a tasting of all East European wines available in this country which I did for *House & Garden* two years ago, the red wine which came second was a Yugoslav wine made from a native grape variety, the Vranac. We couldn't include it in the list of winners because it was only available in two shops at the time. If you see it, try it, and keep some if you like it. Yugoslavian Merlot is very nice too.

Hungary

Hungary's claim to fame is based on one of the great sweet wines of the world, Tokay. There are a number of quality and sweetness levels, and each stage is a real experience. Hungary has also recently attracted some attention for its Merlot, their attempt to follow the Bulgarian lead, usually at around £2 a bottle, at Safeway. It will keep although it's not yet 100 per cent consistent.

Greece

Retsina is a word I write only to forget. Not bad if your senses and taste buds have been blasted into a comatose state by the Grecian sun. Strangely enough Sainsbury's now sell it for people to relive their holidays; there can be no other reason. The Greeks make some good value sweet wines, which are not really for laying down, from Samos, Crete, and the Peloponnese.

Worth keeping are Château Carras, owned by John Carras, who flew the great wine expert Prof. Emile Peynaud from Bordeaux to help him make a quality wine in Khalkidhiki in northern Greece. Other wines are made by John Calliga; Calliga Ruby, and Monte Nero, both made from indigenous grape varieties; not early bloomers.

England

English wines can age, but it is debatable if they will do so to any great effect. The 'problem' of English wine is one of price, they're simply too expensive. They are light, white, refreshing and clean. The best producers are: Carr-Taylor, Biddenden, Lamberhurst and Wootton.

The United States

California is the centre of the American wine industry, and for a long time was the centre of a world technological revolution that has swept the wine industry as a whole. The epicentre has now passed to Australia, but what America does, many other producers start to think about doing.

The famous sunshine is the key to quality wine-making in this state. It makes the grapes fully ripe, and it can be enough of a problem to have motivated the wine-makers to re-think their practices. The largest wine-maker in the world is in California, the Gallo empire which produces 800 million litres of wine a year.

We are the lucky recipients of relatively cheap and good value American wines. What is called neo-Prohibitionism has taken a hold in the US, and many of the wine-makers are unsure how to fight this threat to their livelihoods. I witnessed a fascinating discussion once between Robert (Bob) Mondavi and his son Michael as to the best strategy to use against this threat. Bob thought that all the drink producers should get together, but the son had the wiser counsel. He suggested that the wine-producers should let the spirit-makers fight their own war, and wine should be sold as a civilized part of life.

On 4 May 1976, the English wine-merchant and writer Stephen Spurrier organized a blind tasting in Paris of the best French and Californian wines. He called in the top French wine experts, specifically to give the French a better than evens chance, as this was also PR for Stephen's shop in Paris. The American wines won though. Their more mature fruit was accessible and luscious, whereas the relatively less mature French wines seemed austere and closed.

Things have not been the same since. Anyone who bought a lot of those US wines then will have made a lot of money. Anyone seeking a £/$ currency hedge could think about moving money in and out US wines; but they're perhaps too drinkable to be just an investment and some people have yet to be fully convinced that these wines will profitably mature over the long term.

1966 was also an important year for the US wine industry for two reasons. Firstly Bob Mondavi started up on his own in the Napa Valley, and went on to become the very model of the New World wine-maker. He effectively started a chain of events that now makes California the sixth biggest producer of wine in the world. Secondly, in the Pacific North West, the Eyrie Vineyard in Oregon started planting vines. Oregon will be a large producer of fine wine if the present production is anything to go by. There has been greater attention paid to Washington State of late, and production is starting to take off there. However, at a recent tasting held in London there was a feeling of anti-climax. There are some fine wines, but many that are merely OK.

A tasting of California wines

To start with, a sublimely mature wine that sets an example to follow: Joseph Phelps Syrah, 1981, from Les Amis du Vin, 19 Charlotte St, London, W1P 1HP (Tel: 071-636 4020), at £6.15. Lovely sweet fruit on the nose, a lychee quality, classically balanced, still with some tannin and acidity; lean mature fruit on a throne of complexity and elegance. Buy some.

Some Californian wines to lay down
Cuvaison Winery Carneros
Napa Chardonay, 1987 (£10.25), 1–3 years. Excellent fruit, long, clean and spicy.

*Cabernet Sauvignon, 1986 (£10), 1–2 years. Good tannic structure, very concentrated fruit, rich, and good length. From Anthony Byrne Fine Wines, 88 High Street, Ramsey, Huntingdon, Cambs. PE17 1BS (Tel: 0487-814555).

Pine Ridge Winery, Stag's Leap District, Rutherford Bench, Napa
*Cabernet Sauvignon, 1985 (£12.50), 1–3 years. Good concentrated fruit on nose, long deep fruit on palate, soft and intense, complex and balanced. Excellent.

Pine Ridge are one of the few producers of fine American wines to box their wines in wooden cases. They have found that the American wood they use is too concentrated and doesn't allow the air through, which leads to oxidization of the lead capsules, making them rough to the touch. They recommend drilling a couple of small holes in the sides of the cases. Wholesale by Great American Wine Company, J. O. Sims Building, Winchester Walk, London, SE1 9DG (Tel: 071-407 0502).

Saintsbury Winery One of the new 'hot' names in Carneros.
Carneros Pinot Noir, 1988 (£12), 2–3 yrs. Lovely sweet fruit; slightly flabby on palate, good length, some tannin.

Pinot Noir, 1987 (£10), 2+ years. Slightly short fruit on nose, good acidity, fair tannins and excellent concentrated fruit.

*Pinot Noir, 1988 (£12), 2–5 years. Smoky, full fruit on nose, lovely concentrated fruit, excellent weight, powerful acidity and long soft tannins; rounded and elegant.

Matanzas Creek Winery
*Chardonnay, 1987 (£12.75), 1–4 years. Elegant, restrained fruit on nose. Excellent Chardonnay character on palate, full, soft, austere and spicy. From Hayes, Hanson & Clark, 17 Lettice St, London, SW6 4EH (Tel: 071-736 7878).

Qupe
Syrah, 1988 (£9.25), 1–3+ years. Nice concentrated fruit on nose; lovely fruit on palate, excellent length, full and muscular, balanced with excellent acidity which will carry this wine on. From Morris & Verdin, 28 Churton St, London, SW1V 2LP (Tel: 071-630 7888).

Australia

In terms of value for money, Australia has been many people's favourite for a long time. Prices became very cheap a few years ago when the Australian dollar fell by a quarter in the middle Eighties, at the same time as some large harvests. Since then there have been some bad harvests, and some of the wine-makers, seeing how popular their wines have become, are charging more.

Place names to buy are: Clare, Coonawarra, Southern Vales, Hunter Valley, Mudgee, Pyrenees, Rutherglen, Yarra, and Margaret River. In the Hunter Valley, which is best known for its Chardonnay wines, a grading system has been introduced, with blind tastings to award marks and status. 'Classic' status goes to top wines which are released when mature, and 'Benchmark' goes to younger wines which will achieve 'Classic' in a few years. Another key to quality is the medal which a wine has won; competitive tastings are taken very seriously, and some of the best wines go in for them.

New Zealand

When you can find them, New Zealand wines are excellent although not the bargains of the year. There is a shortage; the producers are planting more vines, and some have put their prices up. Some people's favourite New World Chardonnay and Sauvignon Blanc is Cloudy Bay. There are no bad wines from this part of the world; in the cooler climate of New Zealand, it is easier to produce wine of subtlety and elegance.

South America

South America means Chile first, but now not also last. In 1988 the Masters of Wine visited South America *en masse*, in the same way as they had previously visited Australia. That trip, and subsequent report, assisted Australia's entry to the UK and world wine market. South America is now trying to follow the Australian example. The Torres family from Penedès have been making wine in Chile for a few years, and they went there because of the low costs, and the opportunity to make wine from ungrafted wines, since the phylloxera beetle has not penetrated the region.

One of the largest ranges of South American wines is offered by Bottoms Up, Vintner House, Templefields Industrial Estate, Harlow, Essex CM20 2EA (Tel: 0279-453408). Here are the results of a tasting of their wines:

Chile
Miguel Torres Sauvignon Blanc, Curico, 1988 (£3.49), 1–4 years. Quite nice fruit, clean, sharp, nicely acidic, grassy and good length.

Vina Linderos Cabernet Sauvignon, 1983 (£3.39), 1–2+ years. Nice berry fruit on nose, good soft tannins, pleasant, almost mature fruit. An obvious wine but drinkable.

Mexico
Bodegas Capellania San Carlos Tinto, 1988, Valle de Calafia (£2.99), 1–3 years. 50 per cent Cabernet Franc, mellow tannins, fruit a little thin, hot, full, good finish.

Brazil
Palomas Chardonnay, 1986 (£3.19). Tasting notes read: 'Not clean, little acidity or fruit, pointless'.

Argentina
Estancia Collection, Chardonnay (NV) (£2.79). Very light, clean nose, crisp acidity on finish, good with food, quite good value.

Estancia Collection, Cabernet Sauvignon (NV) (£2.79). Good clean tannins and fruit, nice cedary flavour.

Goyenechea Cabernet Sauvignon, 1983 (£2.99). Very, very pale colour, like the palest Pinot Noir, nose is very hot, with little fruit. Very unusual, Sherry quality, dense and heady.

The Goyenechea Syrah was quite nice too.

Sweet and sticky

A club has now been formed for those who love fine sweet wines, The Sweet Wine Society. Membership is £20 a year which allows you to attend tastings, some of which may cost from £5 extra per session. There is a newsletter and will be visits and offers. To join, write to:

The Sweet Wine Society, P.O. Box 489
London SE17 3DL

Honesty demands I come clean about this plug: I run The Sweet Wine Society.

As a guide to the ten best value sweet wines of the world, I asked Stephen Brooke, author of *Liquid Gold* (Constable), the only book on the subject, for his selection:

1. Sauternes
Ch. Doisy-Dubroca, '83 (Waitrose, £8.95), long keep
Ch. de Berbec, '86 (under £4), quite long
Ch. Bastor-Lamontagne, '86 half bottles, around £4, 2–4+ years.
1985 was not a good year in Sauternes.

2. Loire Bonnezeaux: Ch. de Fesles, '85, under £10, long keep

3. Vouvray Moelleux: by Huet or Foreau, half bottles, −£10, indefinite.

4. Jurançon Moelleux: Domaine Cahaupe, pungent and unique, −£10, indefinite.

5. Banyuls: from Parce, 1969, −£10, long

6. Germany: Riesling Auslese, '76, '83, '85 from the top producers, long keepers.

7. Austria: Beerenauslese and Trockenbeerenauslese, especially Lenz Moser, −£10, very long keepers.

8. Hungary: Tokay Aszu, 5 Putts, '79, '82, around £7/8, indefinite.

9. Italy: Recioto della Valpolicella, from Masi, Tedeschi, Allegrini, £8–12, around 5+ years.
Recioto di Soave, '86, from Anselmi, −£12, 5 yrs.
Vin Santo, from Tuscany, there are many but Brolio is reasonable, −£5, long keep.
Bukkuram Moscato Passito di Pantelleria, from the island of Pantelleria. Dark, intense, raisiny, around £12. Indefinite.

10. Portugal single quinta Ports.
Quinta de Cavadinha, '78, −£14, long keep.
Quinta de Vargellas, −£14, long.
Both are expensive, but cheap compared to the price of 'real' vintage Port.

The best value wines on a restaurant wine list

Some wines never seem to find their way onto restaurant lists, while others seem to be on lots. I asked Michael Edwards, Chief Inspector and wine writer at Egon Ronay's Guides for his ten best value wines that appear on the many lists he sees.

White
1. Sauvignon de St Bris (Fr). Near Chablis, much cheaper. Good growers are Sorin and Very.

2. Bordeaux Blanc (Fr), often very good value and well made; Graves is sometimes a source of undervalued wines.

3. Alsace Pinot Blanc (Fr), esp. from Humbrecht.

4. Crozes-Hermitage Blanc (Fr).

5. Vina Esmeralda Torres (Sp), spicy mixture of Gewürztraminer and Muscat grapes.

6. Australian Chardonnays, especially Balgownie, good versions are very forward and fruity.

Red
7. Chénas (Fr), very good value Beaujolais.

8. Bourgogne Rouge (Fr), especially good value in Scotland, for some strange reason. Try Aubert de Villaine's 'La Digoine', made by the co-owner of Domaine de la Romanée-Conti.

9. Chilean Cabernet Sauvignon, especially Santa Helena, and Santa Rita Medalla Real.

10. Australian Cabernet/Merlots, to go with some more spicy dishes.

7

TASTING WINE

What is tasting?

Tasting is the identifying and measuring of certain known taste co-ordinates; those outlined on page 88, and other, more specific ones. To begin at the end; the finish or aftertaste of a wine is its dominant impression, which is partly chemical debris, and more importantly the memory of the flavour and its shape. Once experienced, it is obvious that it exists, and how long it lasts is an indicator of the quality of the wine. The longer the better.

Tasting wine is an art and a science, and anyone with the use of their senses can learn it. It begins with being able to tell the difference between two wines, essentially by liking one, and not liking the other. The next step is to think why that is so, and the third and final step is to be able to explain that difference to someone else, so that they understand it. Those are the basics.

Beyond this, it starts to get more complicated, but not more difficult, and anyway, no one knows it all. The extraordinary thing about wine is how little we do know about it, especially once it is in the bottle. Tasting wine is about the acquiring of the knowledge we do have, and gaining experience in exercising it, which increases the pleasure of the whole exercise. That, of course, was why we picked up the glass in the first place.

The most important question in the world of wine

Why do two wines made from the same grape varieties, and vinified in the same way taste different, even if there is only a small distance between where they were both grown and made?

Answer: firstly because of the type of soil, and the subsoil; the position facing the sun; the style of viticulture; the microclimate; and finally the immediate environment. If a road was being tarred alongside the vineyard as the grapes were growing, they will take on that flavour, as leaves can ingest significant taste materials from their surroundings. Vine leaves also follow the sun all day, just like sunflowers.

How to do it

The more often you taste, and the greater the range of wines you taste, the more you will learn. Some people form informal tasting groups, each bringing a certain type of bottle, and all learn something cheaply. Like most areas of knowledge, it is a body of practices which have been found to work better than others, and if there are rules, it's because most people keep them.

1. Read the wine, but not the label. Taste blind if you can – cover the bottles up. Don't be distracted, and don't distract others by indicating approval, disapproval, or whatever. Just concentrate on the wine.

2. The eye. Look at the wine in the glass. It should be clear and bright. Tip your glass over on its side, with something white or light behind it; you will see a difference in colour between the centre and the edge of the wine. If the whole is purple with not much difference, then the wine is very young, and if it has brown edges, then the wine is maturing nicely. Really mature fine wines are more brown than red.

3. The nose. Swirl the wine in the glass to disturb the wine and release the bouquet. Don't be too gentle, but don't shake the wine up. Stick your nose in the glass and sniff evenly for three to five seconds. After that time the perception decreases fast, but you can alternate nostrils, or revive your nose with a few seconds out of the glass.

You could be smelling a number of things; fruit, acidity, wood, and beyond these attributes there will be qualities, such as richness, lightness, intensity, blandness. As you breathe these things in, concentrate on what they are saying to you, relaxing your thought processes and just allowing your mind to 'feel' the wine.

4. The mouth. Take some of the wine in your mouth, and taste. Sometimes a wine can be fabulous on the nose, and yet be nothing in the mouth, or vice versa. While it's in your mouth, concentrate again, making sure that the wine is getting to all the parts of your mouth. Different qualities are tasted in different parts of the mouth, so 'chew' the wine around. Open your lips slightly and draw some air across it. You will be making a rather ugly slurping sound when you do this, but hopefully everyone around you is making the same noise. Practise this at home before you do it in public.

The tip of the tongue tastes sweetness, the sides taste saltiness, the edges and the underside taste acidity, and the back tastes tannin.

Concentrate on the impression the wine is making in your mouth, on its profile, and on its character; feel and think.

Then spit, if you want, or have to be professional about it. Practise this at home also. Then ask yourself what you thought.

That is what tasting wine is all about. Not all taste buds taste, and those that do taste different things; if a wine is exceptionally acidic or tannic then don't keep it in your mouth longer than you want to.

The attack   evolution/development   end
2–3 seconds ⟶ 4–10/15 seconds ⟶ ±4 seconds

The three main taste constituents are:

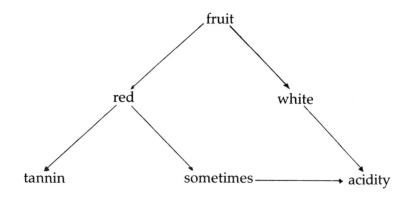

Fruit is the taste of the grape. Acidity can appear in red wines and white, but tannin only appears in red wines, where it can mask fruit. The taste of any wine is in essence a combination of these three units, which can appear in different styles, and in different relative strengths.

Acidity
Some acids come from the grape and these are and taste as follows:
    tartaric – hard
    malic – green
    citric – fresh
while others come from the fermentation process:
    succinic – salty and bitter
    lactic – tart
    acetic – vinegary.

Tannin

Tannins are phenol compounds, or polyphenols and they taste bitter. They give red wine its colour and some of its flavour. Some people are allergic to them, and they can cause headaches; asthmatics especially can have a bad time with them.

Tannin is the ageing agent for red wines; it tastes bitter and dry and abrasive, rather like cold tea. Beaujolais Nouveau is the least tannic red wine, because it has not been kept in contact with the skins, pips, and stalks that give a wine its tannin, and consequently it doesn't live very long in the bottle.

The other source of tannin is the wood the wine comes into contact with, if it is stored in a barrel. These tannins taste dryer, flatter, and not so spirity or muscular as grape tannins. Oddly enough, these tannins can be most clearly tasted in old-style white Riojas which have been wood-aged.

Tasting troubleshooting

What to taste with what?

If you have a lot of very similar wines at one tasting, some of the individual differences can become obscured due to convergence. On the other hand, with too diverse a selection of wine, it becomes harder to recognize characteristics, rather than differences. Try to keep a balance, and order a tasting in gradient steps, of increasing weight or persistence of the wines.

Problems

Tiredness is a common problem during long tastings, because of the intense concentration it requires. Too often people just plough on in a macho way. That's a waste of time and wine. It's much better to take a quick break, and to go slowly, and not worry about 'coming in last'.

In and around the tasting room, anyone attempting to light a cigarette should be shot immediately. Similarly, anyone wearing perfume, aftershave, or even leather should be shown the door. They won't smell it, but you will.

Blind tastings, where the bottle is covered up, are very instructional. Some professionals use these to practise their recognition technique, but the real purpose is to allow each wine tasted to start from the same base line; when done with bottles of very divergent price, it's a useful test of real quality. It is frightening how often we can be so swayed by what we see on the bottle as to ignore or misrepresent what our senses are telling us.

Opening the bottle

First cut the capsule below the collar, and remove it. Below the capsule may be mould or some other unpleasantness. If there should be worm holes then you and/or the place you got it from have a serious problem, if they have spread; check some of the other bottles. Wipe any muck and dust from around the cork or some will fall into the wine as you remove the cork.

Draw the cork. The best implement is the Screwpull 'Lever' and costs £80, but much the best cheaper one is the Original Screwpull; the same company also makes a foil cutter, which is effective on 80 per cent of bottles. Examine the cork: in a red wine, the wine end will be dyed red and it will also be wider. Vintage Port corks must be treated with extra care. The cork may have decayed so far that it may be necessary to use special tongs, which are heated up, worked around the neck of the bottle, and then the top snapped off. Other people do the same trick with a big knife; but they have all practised it. Corkscrews can be used but with maximum sympathy. Sparkling wines should be opened with the bottle tilted as this cuts down on the opening 'whoosh' and waste.

If you want to save a bottle, reseal it with the cork, but don't put the air end of the cork back. Alternatively, use a Vacu-vin.

The glass

There is no perfect amount to pour into the glass. The practical amount is the amount you can safely swirl and tip over.

the best   if you must   waste of time

Paris goblets are used for wine all over the world; they are very ergonomic and stable. Good for drinking out of, but not great for tasting wine from.

The tulip shape/Sherry copita, which has a narrow lip, is too small for the dinner table, but is perfect for leaning on its side to look at the colour, and for concentrating the bouquet released by swirling.

The amount to sip is the practical amount that you can have in your mouth and draw air over without making a mess. Practise it. Practise spitting; the aim is to do it silently, elegantly, but above all, accurately.

Keep going

Nibbles are useful and should be tasteless biscuits or bread. They soak up accreted gunk from your mouth, but also allow you a 10-seconds breather and distraction. There are psycho-physiological reasons for nibbling too. From the point of view of your nervous system, tasting wine excites your taste buds, which in turn excite the brain in the hope that some blood sugars are coming its way; it tells the stomach to get ready to secrete acids and juices to break the food down. It is this unfulfilled digestive action that is responsible for the commonly experienced feeling of intense tiredness after a tasting when there is no food provided afterwards.

The order and temperature of the wines

Start with the lightest wines, go through to the biggest, and end with the sparkling and the sweetest. You will then work through the wines in a way that will not impair your ability to taste successive styles.

It's astonishing how much difference a few degrees of temperature can make. White wine shouldn't be too cold, unless you don't want to taste it. Sancerre is often drunk very cold, which is probably just as well, as in extreme youth it is very acidic. Drink Muscadet at 10°C, Sancerre at 12°C and red wine at 15°C. Sparkling and sweet wines should be quite chilled and very tannic wine warm, as this helps to obscure the tannin – in the same way that cold tea seems more tannic than warm tea.

Writing notes and giving marks

Write the notes you need. Always make sure you can read your writing, and use the words and annotations that make sense to you. Marking wines is a bit of a hornets' nest. The influential American writer, Robert Parker, uses a system based on 100 points, which is common in America, where it is used in schools, and to many people's surprise, starts at 50. 100 is perfect, and he sometimes gives it, while 50 is actually 0.

Some people get very upset about these 'free' 50 points, and prefer the traditional 20-point system. However, if you look at the point range of the majority of 20-point marks, most fall between 10 and 17 points, which effectively is a 7-point scale, as opposed to Parker's effective 50-point scale. Seven points do not allow much flexibility; perhaps 10 would be better – 2 for colour, 3 for nose, 4 for palate, and 1 for luck? But this is not flexible enough, perhaps, to deal with a wine of poor bouquet and great palate. There is no best system, each of the various kinds (and there are many more) have their drawbacks, supporters and detractors. Use the system you feel happiest with, and adapt it as you like.

What is far more important is that if people taste together, they should agree among themselves how they will operate the system they choose to employ. The tastings for this book were conducted under my own system for judging the future of a wine (described later), which worked for the tasters who tried it.

Which words to use
Another hornets' nest. The answer is to use whichever words work for you. The words written about wine are there to convey an impression of the wine, and that's best done simply, clearly, and as strictly as possible. There are around 300 terms used by professionals to describe wine, of which perhaps 20 to 30 are in very regular use.

Structure Wine creates a three-dimensional image in the mind. It can be thick, thin, long, short, even hollow. Wine can be sharp, lean, complete, fat, dense, concentrated, balanced, and graceful and any synonym or opposite of any of the above.

Consistency Wine can be hard, firm, mellow, supple, soft, rich, sticky, cloying, and unctuous; it can also be aggressive, spirity, powerful and fleshy. Carbon dioxide is produced by fermentation and it is possible to feel this as a prickle on the tongue, and for the wine to appear lighter than it really is, especially in a young wine. When it is very pronounced it makes the acidity and tannin more obvious, but it can be dissipated by pouring the wine from one jug to another a few times, which will also aerate the wine.

8

WHAT TO BUY AND WHERE TO BUY IT

How to read the entries

The system used in this book has been devised to award marks for the present quality of the wine, and for its future quality, by giving two scores, both out of ten. They can be added together, but actually it is only the second of the two that is really important.

Next we estimated how long the wine would take to come to its optimum maturity, judged by the level of acidity and/or tannin against the fruit, and as to whether the fruit is a 'tight kernel'. If, say, there is a tight kernel, and the tannin is very heavy, and there is also an impression of elegance and pre-balance (the impression that imbalance will turn into balance), then we have found a winner that will almost definitely repay long keeping. If we don't find that, how far are those qualities absent, and are there any other masking elements (apart from the heavy tannin or acidity) that we could look behind?

Like much else about tasting wine, it is better experienced than explained; once you have tried a few very immature wines, the parameter elements of acidity, tannin and fruit and their overall characteristics will seem clear.

All our tastings have been conducted blind, sometimes with two, sometimes with three of us. The other taster/s did not know the source of the wine, as this information can excite or depress expectations. After each wine was tasted and marked, the bottle was revealed, and then marks for longevity were sometimes revised, in the light of what we know about that type of wine's tendency to age. For example Coteaux du Layon will mature over twenty years or so, but this fact is not fully obvious on the palate.

At the end of the tasting the collected winners, and those we were not sure about, were discussed, re-tasted and rankings agreed, with the final question being, 'Which of those would you really want to lay down?'

A large number of wine companies were asked to send in bottles under £7. Sadly, a few exhibited the 'knaves or fools' attitude, suggesting that all their wines were fully mature – they clearly haven't tasted them. All the shops have submitted free bottles, and only those sent in and tasted under formal conditions have been included in the list that follows; the results of other tastings are in chapter six. Most small shops also sell by mail order.

Of the wines tasted, roughly 50 per cent have got through the sessions, and have been adjudged as definitely worth keeping. Some are certainly better than others, and these quality levels are indicated, but they will certainly all keep very well and improve.

Some of the words used
New World: characteristic of Australia, New Zealand or California, with full, ripe fruit.
Qualities: structure, balance, depth.
General: fruit, tannin, acidity.
Specific fruits: raisins, currants, cherries, peaches, damsons, prunes.
Flavours: oaky, lemony, bricky, gravel, metallic, citrus, toasty, vegetal, stalky, oily, woody, violets, tarry, smoky, coal, herby, berry, flinty, jammy.
Characteristics: forward, baked, spicy, sensuous, bitter, powerful, vigorous, rounded, long, dense, stylish, earthy, complex, light, restrained, racy, ripe, smooth, loose, gentle, sweet, clean, classy, firm, sharp, crisp, inky, big, perfumed, hot, mature, soft, full, warm, accessible, elegant, rich, austere.

All these words mean more or less the same to everyone, and their usage is the everyday sense. Read them, imagine them, think 'wine' and imagine swallowing what you're reading about, and you could be at the original tasting.

Some flavours often associated with specific grape varieties
Cabernet Sauvignon: minty, cigar-box, cedar, blackberries, blackcurrant.
Gamay: bubblegum
Syrah/Shiraz: burnt rubber, brambles
Riesling (mature): petrol
Riesling (young): floral
Semillon: lanolin
Sauvignon Blanc: grass, gooseberries
Chenin Blanc: greengages
Merlot: violets
Zinfandel: black cherries
Sangiovese: cherries
Wines from St. Emilion/Pomerol: leaves

Categories of quality
Best buy: usually one, sometimes two wines, the best wine and the most suitable for laying down sold by this supplier.

Best Value: a wine under or around £4 which will improve into an even better wine.

Good Buy: usually the next best red and white.

Worth Trying: really are worth trying.

* a star means either that this wine is an outperformer; so could be a really good claret, or, it could simply be an exceptional or unusual wine.

√: a tick is one level down from a star.

£: means this is a real bargain wine – very good value.

The key
r – red
w – white
s – sweet

Where they come from
Fr – France
Ger – Germany
It – Italy
Sp – Spain
Port – Portugal
Bul – Bulgaria
Hun – Hungary
Aut – Austria
Aus – Australia
NZ – New Zealand
US – United States of America
Mex – Mexico
Ch – Chile
Arg – Argentina
Leb – Lebanon

VdP – Vin de Pays
NV – Non vintage

Drinking up key
There are three broad time categories for any one wine to be fully mature in: 1 year, 2–3 years, or 5 years. Life is not that simple, of course, so you will also see:

1–3 years, which means that you can drink from 1 year, but you could hang on for 3.

2–3+ years, means that you can drink from 2–3 years, or you could keep it longer, if you have to or want to.

How to read an entry: an example
* Best Buy [clearly good]:

Château XYZ [producer], Graves [region] 1985 [vintage], (Fr) [country of origin], (£6.50) [price at time of tasting], 1–2 years [start drinking 1 year from January 1, 1990, and drink within 1 year] Lovely, rich, elegant, fruit; [first statement is usually about nose, second statement, about palate] good full, rich fruit, balanced tannin, etc.

Recommended wines

Two problems
1. The prices given here are averaged up to the nearest 25p from the price at the time of tasting. Prices may have gone up.

2. Some of these wines may no longer be available and some vintages may have changed. A book needs a long lead time before publication, over six months, and we can only taste what is available. We shall be updating this book and will be able to reduce the lead time.

AVERYS
7 Park St, Bristol, BS1 5NG (Tel: 0272-214141)

Best Buy
r.Château Le Piat, Côtes de Bourg, 1985 (Fr) (£5.50), 1–4 years. Very nice, fruity nose, syrupy and blackcurranty; soft rich fruit, and good firm tannins on palate. Good sound wine, almost ready, but will improve; accessible claret.

Good Buy
w.Nobilo Gisborne Chardonnay, 1987 (NZ) (£7.00) 1–2 years. Warm, honeyed, appley nose; big, gentle, lovely ripe Chardonnay fruit, with a touch of oak, hot, huge acidity, but very well made and will improve a little. Good length and some complexity on the finish.

Worth Trying
r.Rouge Homme Shiraz Cabernet, 1988 (Aus) (£5.25) 2–3 years. Luscious ripe fruit on nose; soft and rich on palate. Touch of vanilla and oak, good kernel of sweetish fruit, some soft tannins.

Berry Bros & Rudd, the oldest wine shop in the world.

BERRY BROS & RUDD
3 St James's, London, SW1A 1EG (Tel: 071-839 9033)
The Wine Shop, Hamilton Close, Houndsmills, Basingstoke, Hants, RG21 2YH (Tel: 0256-23566)

Best Buy

r.*Château Hanteillan, Haut Médoc, 1985 (Fr) (£7.00) 1–3+ years. A classic wine; stylish, stalky, herby nose. Lovely austere, blackcurrant fruit; acidity, some restrained tannin, good weight of fruit. A claret lover's dream. Open the bottle two hours before required.

Good Buy

r.Château de Navarro, Graves, 1984 (Fr) (£6.50) 1–2 years. Clean blackcurrant fruit on nose; ripe rounded fruit, soft tannin; soft and rich fruit on palate, well knit and nice; balanced finish.

Worth Trying

r.Château de la Commanderie, Lalande de Pomerol, 1983 (Fr) (£6.00), 2–4 years. Almost metallic nose, unusual but pleasant. Lots of tannin on finish, earthy and powerful, stalky and quite rich, plummy fruit. Open the bottle two hours before required.

r.Château Plaisance, St Emilion, 1986 (Fr) (£6.75) 2–3 years. Hot, quite pronounced fruit on nose; baked on palate; long soft tannic finish, well balanced fruit is quite vigorous and will develop some elegance.

BIBENDUM

113 Regent's Park Rd, London, NW1 8UR (Tel: 071-586 9761)

Best Buy

w.Gewürztraminer, Rolly Gassmann, Alsace, 1987 (Fr) (£6.00) 1–3 years. Delicious light floral, honeysuckle flavour on nose, SO_2 now present but will fade; light acidity, lots of fruit; concentrated but light. *Pétillant*, fresh, clean, long, lip-smacking finish. Lovely.

r.Rosso di Montalcino, Peiro Talenti, 1987 (It) (£7.00) 2–4 years. Hot, closed nose. Huge tannin, sharp acidity, austere ripe fruit, full and dense; lots of fruit on finish, great depth, nice and big.

Worth Trying

r.Anjou Cabernet, F. Roussier, 1986 (Fr) (£4.50) 1–3+ years. Love it or hate it. Loire reds, and this is representative, have devoted fans and equally vociferous enemies. Stalky, brambly nose; light, pronounced stalky fruit, nice acidity. Some go wild.

r.Bourgogne Pinot Noir, Domaine de la Combe, 1986 (Fr) (£5.50) 1–2 years. Spicy, warm fruit on nose. Really quite acidic and tannic, fruit is a little vague but good weight and length, some complexity. Very drinkable and will become more so.

r.Sangiovetto del Borgo, vino da Tavola, Don Carlo dei Marchesi Citterio, 1985 (£5.00) 2–4 years. Honeyed fruit, full, forward, oaky nose. Lots of tannin, big and soft, some acidity, and a lot of tannin on the finish. Rich and full, almost spirity; will develop into a classy rounded wine.

DOMAINE DIRECT
29 Wilmington Sq, London WC1X 0EG (Tel: 071-837 3521/1142)
Sadly only two wines were submitted, one was perfectly mature, the other was:

w.Mâcon-Viré, André Bonhomme, 1988 (Fr) (£7.00) 2+ years. Open, rich, fruit on nose; smoky (bacon) light, round fruit; already balanced acidity, some elegance.

ELDRIDGE POPE
Weymouth Ave, Dorchester, Dorset, DT1 1QT (Tel: 0305-251251)
Ten branches, one called Godrich & Petman, two called Reynier Wine Libraries.
Cellarage is £2.50 per case p.a.

Best Buy
w.Gundlach Bundschu Sonoma Chardonnay, 1987 (US) (£6.75) 2–4 years. Firm, promising nose; nice oak; hints of a lovely balance of fruit and acidity. Quite acidic now, crisp and some complexity. Could be wonderful.

Best Value
r.Vacqueyras, Côtes du Rhône-Villages, 1986 (Fr) (£4.25) 2–4 years. Hot fruit on nose; heavy, almost stewed fruit on palate, with big tannins, but the certain potential to balance.

Worth Trying
ws.Clos de Ste Catherine, Coteaux du Layon, Raynier, 1986 (Fr) (£5.75) 4+ years. Great potential depth of fruit, firm acidity, good potential balance.

w.Clos du Papillon, Savennières, 1986/7 (Fr) (£5.75) 2–5 years. Short on fruit now, appley nose; very sharply acidic now.

r.Château La Tour St Bonnet, Médoc, 1985 (Fr) (£6.50) 2–4 years. Classic Bordeaux, fleshy fruit on nose. Good full hard tannins, some tarry fruit, light to medium weight.

r.Château Caronne St Gemme, Haut Médoc, 1985 (Fr) (£7.00) 2–5 years. Full, minty Cabernet nose; ripe, full fruit, lots of tannin, will balance very well in the future.

r.*Gran Caus Tinto, Penedès, 1986 (Sp) (£6.25) 2–5 years. Love it or hate it. Dense, hot fruit on nose. Very big acidic, tannic finish, long and medium weight; rich full fruit. Made with the grape varieties of Bordeaux, but tasting radically different.

HUNGERFORD WINE CO.
Unit 3, Station Yard, Hungerford, Berks, RG17 0DY (Tel: 0488-683238)

Best Buy
r.Gran Colegiata Reserva, Toro, 1985 (Sp) (£5.00) 1–2 years. Fleshy, meaty, hot nose; earthy, chocolatey, exotic fruit flavours; good, balanced and hot. Very approachable wine that would be good with food.

Good Value
r.Periquita, 1985 (Port) (£4.00) 1–2+ years. Hot, spicy, raw nose. Thick tannins, good clean fruit, earthy; good weight of tannin to fruit, some complexity.

Good Buys
w.*Wollundry Hunter Valley, Chardonnay 60 per cent, Sémillon 40 per cent, 1986 (Aus) (£7.00) 1–3 years. Peachy, oaky, lovely rounded fruit on nose; tropical fruits on palate, clean and firm, good well-knit acidity, lovely balance, long finish. Excellent and unusual Aussie wine.

r.Cabernet Sauvignon Chantovent Prestige, VDQS d'Oc, 1988 (Fr) (£3.50) 1–3 years. Smoky, attractive fruit on nose. Nice, clean, light; sweet, ripe, young fruit; good light tannin structure.

MAJESTIC WINE WAREHOUSES
421 New King's Rd, London, SW6 4RN (Tel: 071-736 1515)
30 branches nationwide.

Best Buy
r.Stratford Cabernet Sauvignon, 1986 (US) (£6.00) 2–3 years. Powerful minty nose; hot concentrated fruit, firm, but soft tannin on finish; will open out and develop into a very classy, complex wine. 13 per cent alcohol.

Good Value
r.Domaine de Meaux, Cahors, 1986 (Fr) (£3.00) 1–2 years. Full fruit on nose, good fruit, acidity, some sweetish fruit, nice tannin on finish.

w.Vin de Pays d'Oc Chardonnay, Hugh Ryman, 1988 (Fr) (£4.25) 1–2 years. Slightly spicy, soapy nose; OK now. Good balance, sharp underdeveloped fruit, oaky, SO_2.

Good Buy
w.*Chablis Premier Cru, Poinset, 1988 (Fr) (£7.00+) 3+ years. Light

straw, intense fruity nose. Bone dry, good kernel of fruit, good full acidity. Definitely not for drinking now; very sharp and almost bitter. This wine will develop very well and is worth buying into because of the shortage of good mature Chablis.

Worth Trying
r.Wyndham Estate 555 Syrah, 1986 (Aus) (£4.50) now–2 years. Very ripe now, sweet fruit, quite unusual.

r.Châteauneuf-du-Pape, Château Mont-Redon, 1986 (Fr) (£7.00+) 2–3 years. Powerful and concentrated, good clean fruit.

r.Château Meaume, Bordeaux Supérieure, 1986 (Fr) (£4.00) 3+ years. Mellow stalky nose, fiery, steely, big and austere, loads of tannin. Almost undrinkable now, could become very nice.

r.*Château Bertin, 1986 (Fr) (£4.75) 1–3 years. Lots of fruit, and tannin, nicely full acidity. Excellent value for a decent claret.

w.Alsace Gewürztraminer, Léon Beyer, 1987 (Fr) (£7.00) 2–3 years. Very nice and spicy fruit, fair acidity, and good flavour on the palate.

MARKS & SPENCER
57 Baker St, London W1A 1DN (Tel: 071-935 4422)
263 branches nationwide.

Best Buy and Best Value
r.Australian Shiraz Cabernet, 1987 (£4.00) 1–2 years. Good balanced perfumed fruit; hot massive tannin but soft and some elegance, excellent value.

Good Buy
r.*Margaux, 1986 (2nd wine Ch. Brane Cantenac) (£7.00) 1–3 years. Classic perfumed blackberry nose. Very ripe fruit; full, elegant, balanced, austere finish. Very pleasant, complex wine.

Worth Trying
r.Cabernet Sauvignon (varietals – single grape – range) (NV) (Fr) (£3.00) 1–3 years. Elegant ripe fruit on nose; nice, well made fruit, earthy and balanced. Quite good now but will improve for a while. Excellent value.

r.California Cabernet Sauvignon, 1986 (£4.00) 1–2 years. Classic Cabernet fruit on nose. Earthy fruit, some tannin, nicely balanced, mouth-filling; ripe, complete fruit.

MORENO WINES
11 Marylands Rd, London, W9 2DU (Tel: 071-286 0678)
2 Norfolk Place, London, W2 1QN (Tel: 071-723 6897)

Best Buy

r.Santa Rita Cabernet Sauvignon, Medalla Real, 1986 (Ch) (£5.00) 2–3 years. Forward, jammy fruit and oak on the nose; intense, almost overblown fruit, lots of oak and tannin. Easy to enjoy, quite luscious.

Good Buy

r.Vega de Toro, Luis Mateos, 1981 (Sp) (£4.75) 1–3 years. Austere nose, some fruit. A very big wine, high alcohol (14 per cent), lots of tannin and fruit, some acidity, good length and not exactly elegant. Long tannic finish; a big beefy wine.

r.Ribera Duero crianza, 1986 (Sp) (£5.50) 2–3 years. Quite pleasant stalky, cherry nose. Full, rich fruit, vigorous and spicy; clean, good length and good grip.

ODDBINS

31–33 Weir Rd, Durnsford Industrial Estate, London, SW19 8UG (Tel: 081-879 1199)
142 branches nationwide.

Best Buy

w.Ruppertsberger Gaisböhl Riesling Spätslese, 1985 (Ger) (£7.00) 3–5 years. Good acidity and fruit on nose; excellent potential balance; good weight, flowery on finish, and nice acidity. For those who like quality German wines, this will fulfil all their expectations if they have the patience.

Good Buys

ws.Coteaux du Layon, Cuvée d'Adrien, Domaine du Sauvery, 1988 (Fr) (£4.75) 2–3+ years. Good acidity and fruit on nose. Lovely balance of fruit, sweetness and acidity on palate; light elegant, austere acidity that will open out. Could live a long time.

r.Penfolds Bin 28 Kalimna, 1986 (Aus) (£5.00) 2–4 years. Deep colour and harmonious nose. Full fruit, big soft tannins, quite hot attack; still very young but with good ageing potential.

r.Orlando Cabernet Sauvignon, 1986 (Aus) (£4.50) 1–2 years. Lovely ripe Cabernet fruit; rich blackcurrant nose. Good sweet fruit, balanced and luscious; clean tannin on finish and long fruit. A lovely wine, and an archetypal up-front New World Cabernet. 'A friend to all people.'

Worth Trying

r.Château Bertinerie, Côtes de Blaye, 1986 (Fr) (£5.00) 2–4 years. Very oaky nose, minty too; good soft tannic finish and some acidity. Good structure; oak; tannin, and fruit.

r.Cru du Coudoulet, Côtes du Rhône, Perrin, 1987 (Fr) (£5.00) 1–3 years. Full fruit on nose, leafy and vanilla-like. Quite sweet, dense fruit, burnt, and lots of tannin; rich and full with a very tannic finish.

r.Le Pupillo Morellino di Scansano Riserva, 1985 (It) (£7.00) 2–4 years. Oaky assertive, peppery nose. Medium tannic oaky soft fruit; a big wine.

r.Meia Pipa Reserva Especial, 1986, João Pires (Port) (£4.00) 1–3 years. Characteristically raisiny, curranty nose of Iberian wines; woody and rich, not bad balance with tannin and an accessible flavour.

PETER DOMINIC
Astra House, Edinburgh Way, Harlow, Essex, CM20 8EA (Tel: 0279-453408)
800 branches nationwide.

Best Buy
r.Lagunilla Gran Reserva Rioja, 1973 (Sp) (£7.00+) now–1+ years. Lovely ripe, oaky, spice on nose, balanced clean fruit. Delicate raspberry on nose. Perfumed fruit, some tannin on a clean almost elegant finish. Very nice. The '82 may be appearing soon.

Worth Trying
r.Château Lassalle, 1985 (Fr) (£7.00) 1–2 years. An interesting combination of New World levels of ripe fruit, and Old World structure and finesse. Spicy, cedary, warm and oaky fruit. Balanced, clean, firm and good depth of defined fruit; some acidity, ripe and restrained.

CHRISTOPHER PIPER WINES
1 Silver Street, Ottery St Mary, Devon EX11 1DB (Tel: 040481-4139/ 2197)

Best Buy
r.*Château Hanteillan Cru Bourgeois, 1985 (Fr) (£7.00) 1–3 years. See page 98 for tasting notes.

Good Buys
r.Château Musar, 1981 (Leb) (£6.00) 2–4 years. Dense, hot tarry nose; vinous, highly alcoholic (14 per cent), bitter cherries; lots of character.

r.*Vacqueras Domaine le Sang des Cailloux, 1986 (£5.25) 1–3 years. The first wine I've ever tasted that reminded me of the herb basil. Also ripe hot fruit. Lot of fruit and tannin on the palate, some acidity, well-rounded, excellent weight and concentration on fruit. An excellent wine, and very good value.

Worth Trying

r.Shiraz, Brown Brothers, Milawa, 1986 (Aus) (£5.50) 1–3 years. Forward, inviting, cedary nose. A very nice wine; classic fruit on the palate, high alcohol, nice soft tannins.

SAFEWAY

6 Millington Rd, Hayes, Middlesex, UB3 4AY (Tel: 081-848 8744) 500 branches nationwide.

Best Buy

r.Orlando Cabernet Sauvignon, 1986 (Aus) (£4.50) 1–2 years. For tasting notes see page 102.

Best Value

r.Don Darias (NV) (Sp) (£2.50) 1+ year. Astonishing value for a really excellent wine. Very pale colour, very ripe and complex on nose. Ripe, mature fruit, balanced tannin and acidity; hot fruit on a long finish. At £4 this would be not bad value, and at under £2.50, it's a real bargain.

Worth Trying

w.Mâcon Villages Chenu, 1987 (Fr) (£4.25) 1–2 years. Powerful, spicy nose, with oaky Chardonnay fruit. Light fruit on palate, good acidity, good balance and nice weight. Quite austere and a little elegant.

r.*Château de Caraguilhes, Corbières, 1988 (Fr) (£3.50) 2–3 years. Powerful chewy nose. Big tannins, powerful and alcoholic; hot and presently unbalanced. Will cohere and mature into a good value wine. Organically made.

r.Vin de Pays des Coteaux de l'Ardeche Syrah (NV) (Fr) (£2.50) 1–2 years. Good weight of fruit, decent length, and good soft tannin; good fruit on finish.

J. SAINSBURY

Stamford House, Stamford St, London SE1 9LL. (Tel: 071-921 600) 280 branches nationwide.

Best Buy and Best Value

r.Quinta da Bacalhôa, Cabernet Sauvignon, 1985 (Port) (£4.00) 1–5 years. Intensely rich, oaky and blackcurranty on the nose. A lovely wine, with a smooth, rounded smoky oily finish; big and gentle. Very nice now and will improve for some time.

Good Buy

r.Château Burreyres, Haut Médoc, 1986 (Fr) (£4.50) 2–3 years. Austere, classy nose. Stalky fruit, good tannin, long dry finish. A wine for the classic claret lover.

r.*Vino Nobile Di Montepulciano, 1985 (It) (£5.00) 2–5+ years. A big wine; syrupy smooth nose, massively tannic and astringent finish – mouth-puckering and teeth-cracking. Big rounded fruit, dense, clean and bitter. Only masochists would drink this now, but those who know how hard it is to find a mature wine of this kind at such a reasonable price will lay some down.

ws.Clos Saint-Georges, Graves Supérieures, 1986 (Fr) (£4.50) 2–3 years. Lovely, full, luscious almost seaweedy nose. Good ripe botrytis nose, medium acidity and good pre-balance; better on the nose than on the palate, but would cost a lot more if were wonderful on both. Good rich full fruit on finish.

Worth Trying
r.Château Tarteau Chollet, Graves, 1985 (Fr) (£5.00) 1 year. Stalky, jammy nose, some acidity, nice austere fruit; not bad now.

r.Santa Rita Cabernet Sauvignon, Medalla Real, 1986 (Ch) (£5.00) 2–3 years. For tasting notes see page 102.

r.Bourgogne Hautes-Côtes de Nuits, 1985 (Fr) (£6.00) 1–3 years. Powerful, jammy nose; tight tannin and fruit, and slightly smoky on the palate; hot, sharp tannin on finish.

r.*Torres Gran Coronas, 1983 (Sp) (£5.75) now–1 year. Lovely, full fruit, cigar-box nose. Fading tannin, very ripe and mature fruit. This wine could almost count as fully mature, and is a benchmark for what a mature good wine can taste like. Buy a bottle and drink it now. Buy another and keep it 1 year.

r.Saint-Joseph 'Le Grand Pompée', Jaboulet, 1986 (Fr) (£6.00) 2–3 years. Hot, alcoholic fruit on nose; good tannic finish, fruit fades a bit.

r.Châteauneuf-du-Pape, 1986 (Fr) (£7.00+) 2–3 years. Hot, peppery nose; big, soft tannins and some acidity, rich and full, good fruit and tannin on finish.

r.Château Trois-Moulins, Haut Médoc, 1986 (Fr) (£5.00) 2–4 years. Rather closed nose now. Classic claret, good tight fruit, with soft tannins. Very nice.

TANNERS WINES
26 Wyle Cop, Shrewsbury, Shropshire, SY1 1XD (Tel: 0743-232400)
6 branches in the north west.

Best Buy and Best Value
r.*Gran Colegiata Tinto de Crianza, 1986, Toro (Farina) (Sp) (£4.00) 2–5 years. Superb value from a 'new' area in Spain; presently very

cheap and will rise in value fast. Watch out – 14 per cent alcohol. Dense fruit and alcohol on nose; good concentration of fruit; oak, and very full tannins. Fabulous potential for ageing, and a wine with a big future in every sense.

Good Buy
r.Château de Tiregard, AC Pecharmant Comtesse de St Exupéry, 1985 (Fr) (£5.00) now–2 years. Ripe, spicy, summer fruits nose; gorgeous on the palate, rounded, ripe fruit, good balance, nice and firm; clean long finish.

r.Château Macquin St George, AC St George St Emilion, 1985 (Fr) (£7.00) 1–2+ years. Nose rather closed now; a little sweet fruit and leafy. Good, well structured wine, jammy fruit, quite hot, but pleasant now; well balanced and classy.

THOS PEATLING
Westgate House, Bury St Edmunds, Suffolk, IP33 1QS (Tel: 0284-755948)
32 branches in the east.

Best Buy
w.Rully Blanc, Varot, 1987 (Fr) (£7.00) 1–2 years. Very forward rich nose; good acidity, medium fruit, full rounded; very forward acidity, good balance, a nice buttery Chardonnay.

Good Buys
w.Mâcon Viré, Domaine de Roally, 1987, Henri Goyard (Fr) (£7.00) 1–2 years. Quite full acidity and ripe fruit on nose. Lot of firm acidity, clean, good weight of fruit, well made and stylish.

r.Château Lousteauneuf, Médoc, 1985 (English bottled) (Fr) (£4.25) 1–3 years. Very dense, stalky, tarry nose; lots of tannin, both grape and wood. Little jammy, big, dense, and full finish. Fruit a little opaque.

Worth Trying
r.Château Horterie, St Julien, 1982 (English bottled) (Fr) (£7.00) 2–4+ years. Hot stalky, immature on nose. Lot of tannin and acidity, little baked, dense, not showing now.

r.Château de Gueyze, Buzet, 1985 (Fr) (£5.50) 2–4 years. Very full, complete nose, strawberry-like. Lots of tannin, good structure and some acidity; medium dry finish.

TESCO
New Tesco House, PO Box 18, Delamare Rd, Cheshunt, Herts, EN8 9SL (Tel: 0992-32222)
350 stores nationwide.

Best Buy and Best Value
r.Tinto Velho, Alentejo, Reguengos de Monsaraz, 1983 (Port) (£4.00)
1–2+ years. Deep ruby colour; hot fruity nose. Full fruit, good
balance, good soft tannin, nice crisp finish. An outstanding wine for
the price or even at £2 more. Very good now but will carry on
improving.

Good Buys
Fetzer Chardonnay, 1985 (US) (£6.00) 1–2 years. Herby nose; wood
ageing on palate, well knit, fruit still good, full acidic finish; lovely
fruity elegance.

r.Château des Gondats, Bordeaux Supérieur, 1987 (Fr) (£4.00) 2 years.
Robust leafy nose, rich velvet fruit, clear, soft tannin, long full finish.
Classic claret.

Worth Trying
w.Domaine de la Jalousie, 1988, Vin de Pays Côtes de Gascogne,
Grassa (Fr) (£4.00) 1+ year. Clean citrus, woody nose; clean fresh
fruit – perhaps too woody? Crisp finish.

r.*Château Laffitte-Caracasset, St Estèphe, 1985 (Fr) (£6.50) 2 years.
Raw nose; young astringent, good weight, not fully clean, big finish,
very classy; will develop into a classic claret.

r.*Château Léon, Premières Côtes de Bordeaux, 1985 (Fr) (£4.00) 2–3
years. Very young fruit on nose; dense thick tannin, waxy classic
young Bordeaux.

r.*Rosso Conero, Marchetti, 1982 (It) (£4.00) 2–4 years. Huge fruity
nose, scent of rosemary; massive fruit and soft tannin on palate;
lovely rounded finish; with all the herbal qualities expected in an
Italian wine. Very good value for a wine with a difference.

r.Orlando Cabernet Sauvignon, 1986 (Aus) (£4.50) 1–2 years. See
page 102 for tasting notes.

r. Châteauneuf-du-Pape, Les Arnevels, Quiot, 1986 (Fr) (£5.75) 2–3
years. Hot nose; soft rounded fruit, soft tannin, good structure;
complete finish.

w.Alsace Riesling Reserve, Léon Beyer, 1987 (Fr) (£6.00) 2–3 years.
Excellent acidity, strangely oaky on nose, pungent and good.

w.Montagny, 1er cru, 1987, Buxy Coop (Fr) (£7.00) 3 years. Rich
full oaky fruit, good structure, smoky, buttery and firm acidity.
A lovely wine.

THRESHER
Sefton House, 42 Church Rd, Welwyn Garden City, Herts AL8 6PJ
(Tel: 0707-328244)
960 branches nationwide.

Best Buy
r.*Château de Lastours, Cuvée Simon Descamps, Corbières, 1986 (Fr)
(£4.25) 2–4 years. Very deep, young colour. Rich fruit on nose, fleshy.
Very tannic now but with accessible fruit. Quite light fruit, soft
tannins, good potential balance, long vinous finish. An excellent
wine for the price from a property organized as a charity.

Good Value
r.Orianhoritza Reserve Cabernet Sauvignon, 1983 (Bul) (£3.00) 1–2+
years. Little closed on nose; mellow fruit, full long finish, soft
tannins. Austere like a Bordeaux but with rich blackcurrant, plummy
fruit.

w.Khan Krum Reserve Chardonnay, 1986 (Bul) (£3.00) 1–3 years.
Hot, woody nose, reserved fruit. Medium acidity, very woody, little
unbalanced against the fruit, quite tasty, but will improve.

Worth Trying
r.*Torres Gran Coronas, Penedès, 1985 (Sp) (£7.00) 1–3 years. Lovely
spicy, oaky nose. A big, dry Iberian finish, nice weight of fruit, light,
soft tannins; good balance now but will improve. Ripe and peppery.

r.Moulin-à-Vent, La Tour de Bief, Duboeuf, 1987 (Fr) (£7.00) 1–3
years. Hot, cherry nose; very big, medium tannic finish, light fruit
and damsony.

UNWINS
Birchwood House, Victoria St, Dartford, Kent, DA1 5AJ (Tel: 0322-
72711)
300 branches.

Best Buy
w.*Chablis, Bichot, 1987 (Fr) (£7.00) 2–4 years. Closed nose now, a
little smoky, very oaky, good firm acidity; citrus fruit; even an
unlikely flavour of bananas on the finish.

r.Châteauneuf-du-Pape, La Pontificale, 1987 (Fr) (£7.00) 1–3 years.
Quite light for a Châteauneuf; jammy, robust, and quite an elegant
finish.

WAITROSE
171 Victoria St, London, SW1E 5NN (Tel: 071-838 1000)
85 branches.

Best Buy
r.*Hautes Côtes de Beaune, 1986, Caves des Hautes Côtes (Fr) (£5.00)
1–3 years. This wine is almost at its peak now, and will remain in that
condition for a while. Elegant, racy fruit on nose; nicely tannic, good
fruit, and generally an excellent wine for the price. This is the wine to
offer someone who doesn't know what a good Burgundy can taste
like.

Best Value
r.Château Le Gardera, Bordeaux Supérieur, 1985 (Fr) (£4.00) 2–4
years. Classic blackcurrant nose; good hard tannins, sturdy, rich
fruit, long finish. Will develop into a very well priced quality
Bordeaux.

Good Buys
w.*Montagny Premier Cru, 1988, Buxy (Fr) (£7.00) 1–3 years. Beautiful, elegant nose; complex and harmonious fruit and oak. Good long
finish, with sharp acidity, solid structure of fruit; balance on palate
will develop.

ws.Château Bastor-Lamontagne, 1986, Sauternes (Fr) (£4.00) 1–3
years. Lovely, botrytis fruit, full long acidic finish; rich and flowery.

r.Château d'Agassac, 1985, Ludan Haut Médoc (Fr) (£7.00) 1–4 years.
Dense, sweet berry fruit on nose; big fruit, soft firm tannin, hint of
violets, dry finish.

r.Château Musar, 1982 (Leb) (£5.00) 2–4 years. See page 103 for
tasting notes.

Worth Trying
w.Marqués de Murrieta, 1984, Rioja (Sp) (£6.25) 1–3 years. Heavy
perfumed nose; lots of oak, lovely lemony, citric acidity, good
full finish.

w.Mitchelton Wood Matured Marsanne, 1987, Goulburn Valley (Aus)
(£6.00) 1–2 years. Lush and sensuous fruit on nose; good acidity,
some complexity now; fruit, oak and acidity in good balance now,
and will improve.

r.Waitrose Special Reserve Claret, 1985 (Fr) (£4.50) 1–3 years. Sweet
fruit on nose; bitter flavour now with lots of fruit on palate. Good
tannin and once decanted, no one would know it was an own label
wine (albeit a classy one).

r.Savigny-lès-Beaune, 1985, Mommessin (Fr) (£7.00) 2–3 years. Alcoholic nose; rounded fruit and tannin, closed now, will open out and
become balanced.

r.Chianti Classico Riserva Montecastelli, 1981 (It) (£4.95) 1 year. Elegant nose; rich soft fruit, good harmony, long finish, dense tannins, rounded and woody.

ws.Château de Berbec, 1986, Premières Côtes de Bordeaux (Fr) (£4.00) 1 year. Delicate botrytis fruit on nose; good fruit, grapey and firm, low acidity, quite light and peachy.

VICTOR HUGO WINES
Bath Street Wine Cellar, 15 Bath St, St Helier, Jersey, Channel Islands (Tel: 0534-20237)
Other branches in the Channel Islands.
The good thing about living and/or buying wine in this part of the world is the absence of VAT and very low duty.

Best Buy
r.*Raimat Cabernet Sauvignon, 1983 (Sp) (£7.00) 2–3 years. Extremely vigorous nose, leaps out of the glass: sweet warm fruit. Heavy, intense fruit, fat, jammy fruit, some tannin, some acidity. A distinctive wine, nicely balanced between French and New World styles.

Victoria Wine
Brook House, Chertsey Rd, Woking, Surrey, GU21 5BE (Tel: 0483-715066)
850 branches nationwide.

Best Buy
r.*Ser Gioveto, Rocca della Macìe, 1986 (It) (£7.00) 2–4 years. Quite closed now, some full fruit on the nose. Very well knit and well made; some fruit on the finish, hugely but softly tannic, quite drinkable now, but with the capacity to age. A deep well of elegance on which to draw.

Good Buys
w.Kestener Paulinschofberg, Auslese, Mosel, 1985 (Ger) (£7.00) 2–4 years. Nice fresh fruit on nose, some SO_2; light but quite elegant concentrated fruit on the nose; fair bit of acidity and quite good finish. Will blossom.

r.Wynns Coonawarra Cabernet Sauvignon, 1984 (Aus) (£7.00) 1–2 years. Classic cedar/blackcurrant nose, quite alcoholic. Ripe, dense fruit, big and full; medium tannin and some acidity. Quite nice now, but the extra year will allow the acidity to fade away.

YAPP BROTHERS
The Old Brewery, Water St, Mere, Wilts, BA12 6DY (Tel: 0747-860423)
All wines are from France.

Best Buys
r.Crozes-Hermitage, 1987, Graillot (£6.50) 2–5+ years. A very big, powerful wine, alcoholic, burnt rubber nose. A complete wine, soft, elegant berry fruit, big soft tannins, balanced acidity; not cheap now but excellent value in a few years' time.

r.*Domaine Richeaume, Cabernet Sauvignon, Hoesch, 1987 (£7.00) 2–5 years. Classic, minty, woody young nose. A lovely wine; blackcurrant fruit, big and hard now, lots of tannin. A claret with a difference.

Good Value
r.Syrah de l'Ardèche, Saint Désirat-Champagne, 1987 (£4.00) 1–3 years. Earthy, bricky, stalky nose, very forward fruit. Palate not as complex as nose; sweet, ripe fruit, rich and damsony, hard tannic edge. A Vin de Pays that is too young to qualify for AOC status.

Worth Trying
r.Saint-Joseph, Saint Désirat-Champagne, 1985 (£6.50) 2–3 years. Powerful, dense nose, coal-like and stalky. In the palate; hidden fruit, full, hard tannin.

r.Brézème, Cuvée du Grand Chêne, Côtes du Rhône, 1985 (£6.50) 2–5 years. Yes, what and where exactly is Brézème? Tiny production: baked, inky hot rubber nose; very youthful still, austere hard tannins; excellent kernel of fruit, long complete almost gravelly finish. A lovely wine, almost like a Bordeaux.

r.Lirac, La Fermade, 1986 (£5.00) 1–3+ years. Ripe, sweet, almost syrupy fruit on nose. Good clean, soft fruit, some balance; a winter's evening drink with a roast.

YOUNGS & CO.
21 Burnaby St, London, SW10 0PR (Tel: 01-351 1990)

Best Buy
w.Ryecroft Vineyards Chardonnay, 1987 (Aus) (£5.25) 1–3 years. Full blown, oaky fruit on nose. Quite good; lots of soft acidity, a little too much oak now, will soften; ripe fruit, good length; firm and crisp.

Worth Trying
w.Gordon Grant Selection, Sauvignon Blanc, 1986 (Aus) (£4.50) 2+ years. Rather closed nose, some light fruit. Lots of acidity, quite sharp, forward, classy fruit; good weight and length on finish. Good to keep for some time, if the flavour of mature Sauvignon is your fancy.

r.Château Pillebois, Côtes de Castillon, 1985 (Fr) (£4.50) 1–2 years.

Unusual and 'love it or hate it' vegetal nose. Ripe, warm fruit, good acidity, and quite well made.

r.Ryecroft Vineyards Cabernet Sauvignon, 1986 (Aus) (£5.00) 2 years. Light, stalky, alcoholic nose. Good fruit, lots of acidity and tannin, long and full, quite austere, and quite European in style.

w.Fareham Estate, Sparkling White Brut (NV) (Aus) (£5.00) 1–2 years. Good, crisp, nice toasty and strawberry-like. Very high acidity, a little *dosage*, good reachable balance, will improve.

rs.Players Fine Old Tawny, 'Port-style' (NV) (Aus) (£4.75) now+. Not strictly a cellar wine although it will certainly keep; excellent value and delicious soft, sweet, full fruit, prunes, quite luxurious.

Worth a whirl

I am not God, and nor are any of the eight people I've had along to taste with me. We can certainly get it wrong. But while we may on occasion have got it wrong, there were other occasions when we have been unsure. Is this wine hibernating? Will the fruit finally emerge from behind the wall of tannin? And will this currently syrupy soup gain definition and structure? Sometimes we have thought 'yes', sometimes 'no' and sometimes 'maybe'. The wines below are gambles; on balance we would recommend them because although we were not sure whether they would become fine wines, we have certainly learnt a lot about the process of ageing by tasting them. Trying a few bottles would be an investment in education, if nothing else.

Some will definitely come right and develop into classy or distinctive products, while others may fall further into interesting decay or strangeness.

YAPP BROTHERS
r.Gigondas, Domain Saint Gayan, 1985 (Fr) (£6.50) 2–5+ years. Closed nose now, prunes, over ripe. A lot of soft fruit on palate, but with no elegance; full fleshy, almost putrid. Poorly knit and with fair tannin; this wine could be as young as an '88, but more than likely is going through a variant of hibernation, a second childhood. Not a cheap gamble, but quite likely to pay off, and could develop into a wine of immense length and balanced fruit, with a rounded structure.

VICTOR HUGO WINES
r.Château Lestage, 1982, Listrac (Fr) (£6.25) 2–3+ years. Quite syrupy warm fruit on the nose; the concentration of fruit is the problem here. Is it thin and drying out, or is it still overpowered by

the tannin and the acidity? The wine lacks elegance and is a bit short on the finish. Could well come good.

YOUNGS & CO.
w.Château Thieuley, Cuvée Francis Courselle, 1987 (Fr) (£6.75) 2–4+ years. Powerful lanolin nose. Sharp, rasping acidity, presence of fruit beneath; quite sharp and coarse now, but could become very drinkable. After two hours' breathing the nose started to open out to reveal sweet fruit. The problem is the level of acidity, and the quality of the fruit beneath. Could go either way, but will be superb if it comes right, and I think it will.

BIBENDUM
r.Château Belcier, Côtes de Castillon, 1985 (Fr) (£4.75) 2–3+ years. Quite powerful, almost stewed fruit on the nose. Very dry, very forward tannins, but there is a reasonable level of fruit. Finishes rather short and metallic. We feel quite confident about this one.

J. SAINSBURY
w.Eitelsbacher Marianholz Riesling, 1987 (Ger) (£3.25) 1–3+ years. A difficult wine now. Currently some SO_2 on the nose, but lots of acidity, immature fruit and some sweetness. This wine should develop into a decent Riesling, and will be good value for money if it does.

There are other wines that we had strong views about, one or more tasters thinking that they were definitely bad wines, others thinking that they were good. Both sets of tasting notes appear.

YOUNGS & CO.
r.Château Tillede, 1987, Graves de Vayres (Fr) (£5.75) 1+ year.
Bad. Concentrated blackberry nose. Some fruit, but hidden by very bitter astringent nose.
Good. Closed, some fruit on nose. Lot of acidity, clean tannins, good balance, some fruit.

CHRISTOPHER PIPER WINES
r.Château Roquevieille, 1985, Côtes de Castillon (Fr) (£5.50) 2 years.
Good. Short nose, very tannic, good concentration of fruit, quite full and ripe, nice length.
Bad. Muddied, dead nose. Not much fruit, dried up. Quite high acidity, austere and hard. Very tannic finish.

TANNERS
r.Domaine Sainte Anne, Cuvée Notre Dame des Cellettes, 1988, Côtes du Rhône-Villages (Fr) (£6.00) 1–2 years.
Bad. Ribena-like; not much tannin, clean, but light; not much character.

Good. Ripe strawberry, peppery nose; ripe, piercing concentrated fruit on finish.

VICTOR HUGO WINES
r.Château du Cartillan, 1985, Haut Médoc (Fr) (£5.75) 1–2+ years.
Good. Quite tannic, with closed cool fruit on nose. Some acidity, long tannic finish with some well-made balanced fruit on finish.
Bad. Light nose, soft, loose, dull almost musty, short, some acidity.

Three budget cellars
And now to the business end of a cellar: which specific wines to put in it? What follows are three versions within certain price ranges. None of them will suit everyone. This is only a guide, the real idea is to make up your own from the kinds of wine you like among those tasted above.

Cellar A   10 bottles of good wine a year over 3 years – 30 bottles at approx. £5 each = £150.
Cellar B   25 bottles of good wine a year over 3 years – 75 bottles at approx. £5 each = £375.
Cellar C   40 bottles of good wine a year over 5 years – 200 bottles at approx. £7 each = £1,200.

Cellar A
Red
Ch. de Paraza, 1988 (Oddbins/Mistral Wines)
Gran Colegiata, 1988, Toro (Tanners/Oddbins)
Waitrose Special Reserve Claret, 1985
Quinta De Bacalhõa, 1984 (Sainsburys)

White
Vin de Pays d'Oc Chardonnay, 1988 (Majestic)
Domaine de la Jalousie, 1988 (Tesco)

Champagne (Tesco, Majestic, Co-op, M&S)

Sweet/fortified
Ch. Bastor-Lamontagne, 1986, half (Waitrose)
Players Fine Old Tawny (Youngs)

Cellar B
Red
Chianti, Villa di Ventice, 1985 (Winecellars)
Ch. Musar, 1981 (Waitrose/Sainsbury/Christopher Piper)
California Cabernet Sauvignon, 1986 (M&S)
Ch. de Lastours, Cuvée Simon Descamps, 1986/8 (Thresher)

White
Mâcon Villages, 1987 (Safeway)
Rully Blanc, Varot, 1987 (Thos Peatling)
Montagny 1er Cru, 1987 (Tesco/Waitrose)
Gordon Grant selection Sauvignon, 1986 (Youngs)

Champagne
Eldridge Pope Chairman's

Sweet
Jurançon Moelleux, 1988 (Oddbins)

Cellar C
Red
Ghiaie della Furba, Cappezzana, 1985 (Winecellars)
Firestone Cabernet Sauvignon, 1986 (Les Amis du Vin)
Ch. Hanteillan, 1985 (Berry Bros/Christopher Piper)
Crozes-Hermitage, 1987, Graillot (Yapp)

White
Alsace Gewürztraminer, Gassmann, 1987/8 (Bibendum)
Gundlach Bundschu Sonoma Chardonnay, 1987 (Eldridge Pope)
Wollundry Hunter Valley, 1986 (Hungerford)
Chablis, 1er Cru, 1988 (Majestic)

Champagne
Charles Heidsieck

Sweet
Kestener Paulinschofberg Auslese, 1985 (Victoria)

9

WINE AS AN INVESTMENT

Investing in wine is a relatively safe form of investment, at least over the long term. But for people for whom wine is about drinking and pleasure rather than profit, wine investment is a Great Evil, because it has pushed up the prices of the finest wines so that today they are hugely expensive.

The glance down the right-hand side of the wine list in a restaurant is a common feature of the business lunch. The Japanese apparently always stick to a budget, while the Americans want to power-spend, just to show that they can. Other motivations are chauvinism and greed. But fine wine is a secret in a bottle. It is also very different from a Van Gogh because it can only be appreciated once, and it is a waste if it is underappreciated.

So, what is this wine investment that people get so worked up about? It began in the late 1960s when American investors started to move in. It grew fast and then hit the floor in 1973–74. Some older wine-lovers still talk wistfully about the bargains they picked up then. The market has wobbled along since. The strength of the US dollar is the key to its direction, as more or fewer Americans enter the market according to how cheap or expensive these wines are to them.

Investment is not intrinsically bad if it is done to finance current drinking or future buying. But investment purely to make money, otherwise known as speculation, can be seen as a bad thing because it affects the market. It is also, of course, unstoppable. So far. If you must do it, here's how. The basics of financial commonsense apply: spread your risk – don't buy only one kind or vintage of wine, buy the best, because people will always want the best; buy from trustworthy and reputable people; the amount of money you put in depends on how deep your pockets are, but the more you do put in, the greater the return, taking into account also that storage and dispersal costs will eat relatively more into smaller sums; don't invest more than you would like to spend on wines to drink, should it come to that.

The index of price rises of the best Bordeaux, on the *Decanter* index of combined wine prices, just like the FT index, starting in August 1978, shows a rise of 525 per cent to August 1989, while the FT30 Share index shows a 325 per cent rise over the same period. Since 1974, it has been very hard to lose money on wine, and things now look so rosy that there is even a specialized company that is starting to invest in fine wines, called Russell Sharp and Russell. A few years ago a lot of money was pumped into the market once accountants realized that BES (Business Expansion Schemes) designed to offer tax-free investment funds could legitimately invest in it. That has changed now, but there are plenty of formal and informal syndicates that still invest, even some merchant banks. Some people in the trade have made a lot of money advising these investors, although that information is easy enough to come by, as most specialist merchants hand it out for free, in the hope you buy the wines from them.

All is not gold at the end of the rainbow, however. It is certainly possible to lose a lot of money on wine, especially if money alone is the reason for investing. One wonderful story concerns the most expensive bottle ever sold, a Château Lafitte – as it was spelt then – from 1787, sold in 1985 for £105,000 at Christie's to the late super-rich publisher Malcolm Forbes. The bottle was believed to have once been the property of Thomas Jefferson, ex-President of the United States. Bought as a publicity vehicle for the buyer, it was put on display, upright, under bright lights, which caused the cork to dry out and fall into the bottle, thus making it practically worthless. 'Gotcha', as *The Sun* might say.

Many who bought the much-vaunted '82 clarets could now sell for less than they paid for them; some are now cheaper than they were in 1985. What about 1988? I would say buy, but only what you want to drink. It is a very tannic year, and not with great finesse. Right-bank properties, from St Emilion and Pomerol will mature faster, so they may be better. The best wines of 1988 were the sweet ones, so Sauternes-Barsac is the only real buy. Rhône wines had a very successful year in '88, and can be considered. At the time of writing, '89 seems a more successful year, but only if the price is right and it probably won't be.

The way to buy these wines *en primeur* is to get on the mailing lists of the merchants and to watch the prices in *Decanter* and *Wine* magazines, as there will be some variations. This is one of the few times that merchants compete in an open market on price, so if you think one is charging too much, say so, and move on.

Vintage Port is the easiest market to find your way around. There are a few great names – Taylor especially, Graham, Dow, Warre and Fonseca, and some nearly great names behind them. The Port market is very small compared to the Bordeaux market, and American investors have become interested in it lately, which has pushed up prices. The market moves very differently from other markets also, because it moves along quietly until the wine is ready to drink, and then the price goes up very fast. The reason for this is that there are not many people who want to hang onto Port for twenty years, even those who want to drink it.

What makes the Port market safer than any other fine wine market is the control the producers have over it; they can release more or less wine to keep the price stable.

Which is very different from the outlook for Burgundy. The Burgundy market is of a similar size to the Port one, but it is almost the complete opposite. Here the wines can vary in quality a great deal, depending on the vintage conditions. Apart from the top names, there is a minefield of specialized knowledge about which wine-makers are really worth buying. My personal view is that, because of Japanese interest, the top Burgundies are the only exception to the 'spread your risk' rule; buying a few parcels of top quality wine may prove a good investment.

Beyond the normal buying of fine wine, some investors adopt strange strategies, such as buying the whole set of Mouton-Rothschild with artist-designed labels, starting from 1946. It is also possible that corkscrews have shown a greater appreciation over the last ten years than wine itself has. The International Society of Corkscrew Addicts exists for such enthusiasts.

One of the main attractions of investing in fine wine is that it does not attract Capital Gains Tax. As long as the taxman does not suspect that you are 'trading' in the wine, you are free and clear, because wine is defined as a 'wasting asset' – i.e. the longer you have it, the less it is worth. The same is true for vintage cars.

Christie's Wine Department was the first and is still the largest auctioneer of fine wine. I asked Duncan McEwan, a Director, about the current market for wine. He thinks that the best value of any wines are the German ones; '1971 Auslese and Spätlese are £5 a bottle at auction, that's fantastic value'. It seems hard to recommend keeping these wines, but very easy to buy them at auction, and drink them. The real reason why these wines are so cheap at auction, Duncan believes, is because in Britain we don't know when to drink them. He recommends treating them as an aperitif, so their sweetness won't interfere with food.

The small punter can operate in the *en primeur* market, he believes, so long as the money is put in for a while, and not necessarily with a view to re-sale. 'Some things are very cheap, partly because some other things are very expensive. Some people come along and want to spend a lot of money to buy '66 or '70, that are ready to drink now, a Lafite at, say, £700–800 a case, but an '86 is about £400, so for that price differential, why have something that somebody has paid to keep for 20 years? Port is different, the trade is not prepared to put its money into Port. So the '83s and '85s are on the market, and we have people who want to sell their Graham '83 at about £120, while the '85 came onto the market at £140/150. Both are cheaper now than when they were *en primeur*. It's crazy to sell for less than you bought for.'

The individual who wants to put £500 to £1,000 into Port, has to reckon to keep it there for ten years at least. Duncan recommends the '83s as the ones to buy, and has 'lots and lots' himself. Bordeaux accounts for 70–75 per cent of what Christie's sell; the rest of the market is divided equally between Port and Burgundy. A small but growing sector has been vintage Cognac, which Duncan believes is not cheap any more. Considerable hype attended a recent sale of vintage Armagnac but that did not go well, and this market does not seem ripe for safe investment.

'The thing is this, to have investment, you've got to have consumption. That's the key to all this', Duncan believes. 'You've got to have a diminishing supply, because there are vintages coming along all the time. Bordeaux in the '80s has produced seven or eight good or excellent vintages, and even the lowlier ones, '84 and '87, are moving up in price now. So there has to be something coming out the other end – people drawing corks.'

The price of claret vintages goes through strange changes and realignments. 1980 and 1981 were completely overshadowed by the arrival of the 1982 and then the 1983 vintage, which spread a cloud over the prices of most of the '80s vintages. The last couple of years have seen an evening out of these unjustified differences as some of these wines have become seen as good value for drinking. Fashion among châteaux also plays its part, some moving up, others moving down, and then whole regions enter the limelight, in the way Pomerol did.

From the point of view of investment, the best châteaux of certain vintages become the core market leaders. ' '82 has become like '70 and '61 before it, the backbone of the market, the top price of the decade. The '61 prices are peaking now as they approach full maturity. On the other hand '85s are receding into Cinderella-hood as they become overshadowed. It's not as good as the '82, and it's not drinkable like the '83 and '86. But '84 is a wine that is almost unsellable at auction, and very, very cheap. It won't mature much, if at all.

119

'Very off-the-boil in market terms are Calon Ségur and Lynch Bages '64, two well known wine disasters, along with some châteaux, like Gloria, Cissac, and Château Clark, a Rothschild operation that apparently has ceased production. On the way up, I suppose, is Chasse-Spleen, but I have my doubts about the arrival of Fronsac. A good value tip might be Château Le Terte-Rôteboeuf, often around £7 a bottle at auction, a classic St Emilion, delicious.'

Fashion is behind the leap forward in the price of some very small production Rhône wines of the highest quality. Wines such as Le Mouline and La Turque '85 sell for £2,500 a case, as much as Pétrus, and there were only 333 cases of La Turque made that year. Those prices are the result of pure speculation. The wine is great and stupendous, but, arguably, no wine is worth that sort of money as a drink, only as an investment.

Duncan's good-value areas are Bulgaria, Rioja, small Bourgeois growths in Bordeaux, south-west France, Provence, Northern Italy, Eastern Europe and especially Chilean wines, are all among his own house plonk, and Australian and New Zealand white he considers to be better value than Californian. 'We're spoilt for choice.'

His tip for good value at auctions is to bid and bid, and bid again. Around 70 per cent of the lots at Christie's are covered by left, or commissioned bids, and their failure rate is very high, around 90 per cent. But that leaves 10 per cent of left bids succeeding in buying wine at a very reasonable price. It is well worth doing. Exceptional sales will usually produce exceptional prices, but the bread-and-butter market depends upon people leaving realistic bids, and the habit is worth cultivating.

Michael Broadbent's view of the Port market echos Duncan's. Just returned from Tokyo, his view of the market in general had a wider perspective, and was somewhat melancholic. 'The current state of the Port market is edgy; there is a danger of its going up in price, and becoming overpriced, because the American market has become so big. They don't quite know what to do with it over there, but they buy it. They're drinking it far too young, and they only want a vintage. The problem is that they've never had the convention of laying wines down.

'Actually, yes, if some people wanted to put some money aside, they should buy vintage Port for eventual resale to the American market. The '85s, rather than the '83s I think. I'm not sure who's drinking it, but we sell a lot. At the moment I think prices are high enough, because currently it translates to £400 for a case and that's quite expensive enough for a glass in a club. That's the thing

Michael Broadbent.

about wine, the more that's drunk, the less there is left to drink, so it's got built-in inflation.

'What does worry me is that the Japanese are coming into the fine wine market, pricing even the Americans out. But it isn't as if it's a part of their lifestyle, and it doesn't go with their food, but the rich are going to buy the best. We've had a client who had $40 million to invest in wine, which distorts the market, because they only want the top growths.

'The Japanese are most interested in Burgundy, in Romanée-Conti and Montrachet; they'll pay anything for it, so unless you're amazingly rich, those wines are out for you. I wouldn't advise anyone to buy Château Pétrus, but we sold a whole load of it recently, '79, '81, '82, '86 all bought by a merchant banker *en primeur*, and he made a huge capital gain.

121

'Actually we like people who buy for drinking, but I suppose that's slightly hypocritical, because we're in the business of selling wine.'

Michael is a great supporter of Madeira. 'Yes, I love Madeira. But another great unsung wine is the Australian liqueur muscats from north-east Victoria. They don't have the acidity of Madeira but they have the richness and tang. Tokay also can be really beautiful, again tangy and fairly high acidity, and extremely good value. The top ones go for £50 a bottle, but that's nothing compared to Sauternes. Madeira is also very good value, from £15 up to £300 for a genuine 1789 bottle. Otherwise it's around £75. The great advantage about Madeira and Tokay is that you can keep it open for some time, as we have here, [drinking that delicious 1839 still] just with the cork in, in the fridge. You can't do that with Port.

'The German wine market is so complicated. They've completely mucked up their wine laws, no one can find their way round the maze. It worries me.'

For the last word on investment we return to John Armit for the pure money view. John has run a wine investment organization for a while, with some very large players involved. 'On the whole wine investment is a very good idea. But you have to know what you're doing. Some people know what they're doing, and I do. £5,000 is the minimum. Then certain things need to be borne in mind. First, it's not liquid investment, despite its nature. It's not something you should borrow money to do, and it should be only a part of a portfolio. I can see no reason why the top twenty-five châteaux shouldn't continue to appreciate. They produce five million bottles a year on average, that seems like a lot, but it's being drunk all the time.

'You can build up a serious cellar over fifteen years. For example, £10,000 invested in 1970 would be worth £260,000 now. But the best idea is to go in once, and as opportunities arise, sell it off and buy more. If you've really only got £500 or £1,000, then buy the very best châteaux *en primeur*. I believe '88 will be a good investment; '86 was, '87 wasn't, '82 was, '83 was, '85 was all right but they'll need longer. '89 will probably be expensive.'

John is unconvinced that sweet wines are a good buy at present prices, and is unremitting in his criticism of the Port market. 'Vintage Port is clearly not a drink of the twentieth century. It's of limited quality and of limited interest. I have no belief in the market, because I know so few people who drink the stuff. It's being sustained by collectors in the US, but I'm not sure they're drinking it. The trouble with vintage Port is that you don't feel good the next day, and my advice to people with vintage Port is to sell it.' I did get him to agree, reluctantly, that the vintage declaration mechanism which allows the producers to regulate the amount of vintage wine released, at least removed the downside from the market; 'yes, but I don't just believe in that market'.

He doesn't think much of Burgundy from that point of view either. He likes drinking it, and suggests the areas of Rully, St-Aubin, the Côte Chalonnaise, as being very good value, and definitely due for price rises; a 'drinking buy'.

John thinks Fronsac and Canon-Fronsac are under valued. 'They are not of the quality of the top Pomerols, but they are very well priced. They are very drinkable, plump, ripe young things.'

Two other investment vehicles have appeared recently; Port futures in the real sense and shares in vineyards. Advanced Port Purchases (APP) are being sold by a small family concern called La Rosa through Dourosa Investments, their subsidiary. £1,000 buys five cases of Quinta de la Rosa over 5 years, which can be surrendered for 4 cases of mature tawny Port. That would be pretty expensive tawny. La Rosa project that with 4 reasonable harvests, and one vintage year, a 16 per cent p.a. growth rate is likely.

Alternatively, Henry Ryman has been selling 250 wine bonds at £2,500 each. Originally sold in 1980, each pays interest of ten cases of wine for five years, a total of 600 bottles of Château La Jaubertie in the Dordogne. After five years the bondholder receives back the money, or twenty-five cases of wine, or re-invests.

Someone else has jumped on this bandwagon, but with a difference. Andrew Gordon started Wineshare in 1986 when he bought a château in the Dordogne. Investors paid £380 for a row of vines and were guaranteed thirty cases of wine when they started producing (three years after). Over 400 investors have taken him up. They can take less or no wine, and have to pay extra for bottling, shipping and duty, giving a bottle for around £2.30 in 1991.

Buying and selling at auctions

If you want to buy mature wine, one of the places to do it is at auction. The first thing to do is to get on the mailing lists (see later for addresses). You can bid by post also. Various arcane terms will appear in the catalogue, such as 'Duty paid' which means that the paid duty can't be claimed back by an overseas buyer. 'In bond', means you will have to pay duty on it, and 'duty paid available in bond' means either option is possible depending on whether the buyer is from the UK or overseas. VAT is added at 15 per cent to lots sold by VAT-registered sellers, indicated by a dagger beside the lot number. 'FOB' means 'Free on Board', which means that the wine is abroad, adding shipping costs to the final price. 'Ex cellar' means that the wine is still at the cellar where it was made, the best conditions it could have lived under, and adding a premium to the price.

Each lot is numbered and lots can consist of single bottles, multiple cases, or mixed cases. Bidding goes up by single pounds until £50, and progresses by bigger stages after that. Add 10 per cent or 15 per cent to the final price, the 'hammer price', for the buyer's premium.

The one rule

Never pay more than you wanted to pay before you walked into the auction room. At the risk of appearing dull, I'll repeat that in a different form: don't allow yourself to get carried away by the heat of the moment and pay £150 when, ten minutes earlier, you thought Lot 36 was only worth £120 to you. You were right the first time. There will always be other bottles, and other auctions, when you really will get the bottles you want, and cheaply, so save your money till then.

If you want to pay £120 for Lot 36, don't jump in at £120 with a bid. If the price is moving up in £10 stages, start at £100. Someone may bid £110 against you, and you can then bid £120. You might even get it for £100.

Selling at auction is very similar to buying at auction; the uncertainty lies in the price each lot will make, though you can put a reserve on your wine. In general, this method is not for the impatient; it could be a while before you see your money.

Bring your own back alive

Continental Europeans know some pleasures that are mostly foreign to these shores. One, of course, is drinking wine without ridiculous duties attached to it. Another is visiting vineyards.

We have started to pick up the habit; more and more people tour English vineyards, and if you go to France, don't you want to bring some wine back with you? The trouble is only worth going to for decent wine, so if you do find something very good, make the effort.

When you get to the winery, look around. Are there bits and pieces everywhere, and is the place pretty mucky? If so, go. Good wine-makers take a pride in their surroundings and their wine, and bad habits in one aspect will likely translate into the other.

Car boots are better than roof racks for storing wine, but not by much, being havens of heat, vibration, and fumes. Store the bottles anyhow, since it will not matter if the wine is not in contact with the cork for a few days. Wrap the boxes in something, such as newspapers or cloth, that will stabilize the temperature, and allow the bottles to recover when you get them home. If you are flying, it is better to take the bottles on the plane as hand luggage.

HM Customs and Excise are very interested in people who bring alcoholic beverages into the country, as they tend to view these people as money making opportunities for their Department. If the wines come from an EC country the personal limit is ten and a half 75cl bottles per person over eighteen assuming that you take all your alcohol allowance as wine and do not bring in any spirits or sparkling wines. If you do bring in spirits or sparkling wine, your allowance is six and a half 75cl bottles. Beyond that, you must pay duty of 95 pence per bottle and VAT on the purchase price, so keep the receipt.

This will still save you some money, if you choose the right wine. At some point, however, while looking at the dozens of cases piled up on your car or in your van the Customs man will stop believing that this wine is not for re-sale, and that means problems, so find some way of convincing him. Or:

How to import your own

Ask anyone who has done it and the first thing they will tell you (and they're really not joking) is:

1. Don't do it.

2. Get some samples sent or visit the region and taste. Always take two bottles back with you and re-taste in Britain.

3. Steam off or get duplicates of the label, neck label and back label and send them to one of the nine regional inspectors with the Wine Standards Board; they will have to approve them regarding EC regulations. The Head Office is at 5 King's House, 1 Queen Street Place, London, EC4R 1QS (Tel: 071-236 9512).

4. Re-think what you're doing. If you are going to re-sell the wine commercially, rather than to friends, you will have to move great volumes if the wine is a cheap one.

5. Agree terms with the seller, either thirty or sixty days for full payment by banker's draft (cost £7.50), and confirm exact details of order in writing.

6. It's easier to effect entry, organize documents, and many other things if you arrange for a forwarding agent to pick the wine up for you and bring it to a bonded warehouse or wherever in the UK. Charges are between £2 and £10 a case.

7. Using a bonded warehouse will allow you to avoid paying VAT and duty until the wine is cleared, otherwise it is due immediately on landing.

8. Sell it; if you do this commercially, you may have to wait thirty to sixty days yourself for payment. The profit margin is very poor, around 20–30 per cent of the purchase price, giving you a mark up of 15–20 per cent. That's not a lot.

9. Build into your costing 10 per cent for breakages and currency fluctuation.

Canny investors, and all people in the wine business, store their wine at bonded warehouses. The problem at some bonded warehouses can be a lack of efficiency and wine knowledge, which can lead to disastrous muddles. For example, wine merchant X sends a fax to the warehouse to send a case of Château La Fleur-Pétrus (the neighbouring property to Ch. Pétrus, worth £220) from his stock to merchant Y. The warehouse by mistake dispatches a case of Château Pétrus (worth £2,200). If merchant Y is honest he will tell merchant X, but that wouldn't happen very often.

A bonded warehouse is really only as good as the local Customs & Excise inspectorate who keeps tabs on it. In London there are vigorously enforced regulations on the size of the holes in the wire separating in-bond from unbonded wine, so that half-bottles cannot be passed through. There are other parts of the country where that division is marked by a chalk line drawn on the floor. Sadly not all such places are fully vigilant about keeping bottles horizontal. So always visit any bonded warehouse you are planning to use, and follow their progress closely.

They are certainly worth using, because they will save you money. While your wine is there you will not have to pay duty or VAT. More importantly, when the wine leaves the warehouse you only pay VAT on the purchase price, not on the sale price, which, if the wine has appreciated by 300 per cent over ten years, will represent a pretty big saving.

The largest privately-run, temperature-controlled wine cellar in the world, is owned by the Wine Society. The Society has just opened a huge warehouse in Stevenage where the Society's own and Member's own stock will be kept under perfect conditions, at 50°F and in the dark, for most of the time. As described on page 41, the system is very space efficient, storing twenty-four bottles, neck on neck, in bins built out of Dexion Racking. They had to move 100,000 cases of wine (1.2 million bottles) into the huge new building that will cost the

Society the staggering sum of £4.5 million. That's a lot of bottles and a lot of money.

The Society delivers wine to its members as well as holding it for them, although some members have odd delivery problems. One woman asked that the wine be left in the dustbin except on Mondays, when the dustmen came, as she was out at work during the day. Another gave the door key to the driver so he could deliver the wine directly, and yet another had an imitation dog kennel built, just for wine deliveries. At present the cost of cellarage at the Society is £3.60 per case p.a. and it is now available to non-members. Anyone for whom storage is a real problem, and who has some wines worth serious storage should consider using this facility. The Wine Society, Gunnels Wood Road, Stevenage, Herts SG1 2BG (Tel: 0438-741177).

HOW TO SERVE WINE

W e come to the part when the pleasure really begins, and the whole point of this book: getting pleasure from drinking wine. Most wines are best decanted, but the most common errors, which don't show wine at its best, are serving it at the wrong temperature (white wine too cold, red wine too warm) and pouring it into the wrong kind of glass.

Most white wines do not require 'breathing' (allowing the wine some contact with the air) although I have found that an Italian white wine, Lugana, does benefit from this. Generally, the bigger the wine, the longer it should breathe.

Decanting is important especially if the wine (usually red) has thrown a sediment. Light a candle and hold the bottle close to it so that the pile of sediment is visible as you pour the wine. Sediment is quite harmless. The only problem is that it stops you drinking the last of the wine in the bottle. .

There are two views about what to do with very old wine. Michael Broadbent used to think that very careful handling and immediate drinking was the rule for very old wines, but he has seen very different treatment work as well. Emile Peynaud, the great Bordeaux oenologist, on the other hand, has seen old wine turn to vinegar in the decanter. It probably comes down to the condition of the wine. If it is very stable and has been handled properly all its life, it will be very resilient, otherwise, not. Another little disagreement exists between those who think that vintage Ports should be left open for twenty-four hours so some of the alcohol can evaporate, and others, the majority, who do the exact opposite.

Temperature is the most important factor affecting the taste of wine. A red wine served at 70°F will taste flabby, alcoholic and flat, but if it is too cold, it will display its tannin. Bouquet is the key indicator; if it is short and closed, but the wine mature, then it is possible the wine is too warm or cold. Quick remedies are to put the bottle on the floor to keep it a little cooler, or to warm the wine in the glass by cupping it in your hands. Beaujolais can be put in the fridge, as can cheap Valpolicella, because the very low levels of tannin will not make the wine taste nasty when chilled. A strange feature of wine that has been opened for some time, even of tannic red wines, is that chilling in the fridge seems to dampen down the tannin or certainly the alcohol, allowing the fruit to seem more prominent, perhaps something to do with partial oxidation.

The warmer a white wine is, the worst its faults seem to be. This has turned into a fetish for chilling all white wine, however good, as cold as possible, which is a waste. It takes one to two hours to chill a bottle of wine in the fridge, depending on how full the fridge is, and how often the door is opened. It will take longer in fridges that are too warm, which apparently is most of them. Pop your thermometer into the fridge for a while to see how un-cold it really is. 0°F should be the target. You can chill the bottle faster in the freezer, but don't forget it, and even better is iced water in an ice bucket, where ten minutes will chill it pleasantly. The perfect solution is a cold mountain stream, but most of us don't have one of those handy.

If you want to warm a wine, red or white, the quickest way to do it is to put it in the microwave. Honestly. Twenty-five seconds is fine, and it will not affect the taste.

Wine glasses and soap are not natural bedfellows. Clean glasses should be stored the right way up, or odours could be trapped underneath. If soap is used then the glass should be rinsed properly, preferably in pure mineral water. If it is dried, then the cloth should be perfectly clean, and not a bleach-sodden rag as happened at a tasting I attended once.

Washing-up liquid, and its residue will kill Champagne, so if you are celebrating, make sure the glasses are squeaky clean. If a decanter becomes stained it can be left overnight with water and denture cleaner in it, then rinsed thoroughly.

The glass you drink your wine from shouldn't be huge or tiny, and ideally slightly tulip-shaped to concentrate the bouquet. It should be clear, as cut glass looks very nice in itself, but doesn't show off the wine to best advantage.

If you have some wine left over you can use a Vacu-vin pump to make a vacuum between the wine and the rubber stopper. The Vacu-vin is not quite the wonder it is claimed to be. It doesn't seem to work with Burgundy, or with wines which have a fair bit of carbon dioxide, which you can see when you pump, because a froth forms on top of the wine. A cork is best with these wines, and best of all a half bottle you have saved for precisely this occasion, and that will keep for a week or so.

Wine books often talk about matching food and wine. I have always found this to be a frustrating and immensely complicated exercise. It is extraordinary, yes, how some flavours can complement each other, but bizarre, also, how some things can be insisted on by some writers. There is a lot to be said about this subject, but this is not the place for it. If it tastes good to you, and you have had the taste to get this far, go ahead.

Postscript

Wine, like anything else that is worthwhile in life, is worth getting organized about. The more people you organize, the greater the buying power harnessed, and the greater the benefits. If you have no space to store wine, find someone who does and come to an arrangement with them. Another possibility is to store your wine with a wine merchant. This is only worth doing in the long term. Charges range from £2 per case per year, to around £5. Always visit the site and look it over, ask difficult questions about temperature, temperature swings, humidity and anything else you fancy. Then pick the nearest decent one to where you live.

If your wine is going to live with someone else on an informal basis, try to achieve some peace of mind by locking it up. Mention the possibility of children stealing bottles; some parents get worked up about this, but others take a more realistic view. If that fails, suggest burglars, and the now very high incidence of bottles going missing along with the video and jewellery – bottles being quite untraceable, of course. What you want is a sturdy wire mesh fence with a lock and key. And then you are set up and ready to go.

What you will be doing then is getting more out of your bottles. You will be drinking better bottles of wine for less money, by keeping them yourself. You will also be making the most of a civilized and complete pleasure. Drink better wine by keeping it and we shall all be happier.

Appendix 1

Twenty things you might like to know about wine

1. La Romanée-Conti is the most expensive wine produced today. The top selling vintage is 1945, which could sell at £9,000 <u>a bottle</u> (in Tokyo).

2. Wine has been made for around 7,000 years and, possibly, started in Georgia in Russia.

3. The most expensive corkscrew was sold at Sotheby's in 1985 for £4,620. It was a bronze nineteenth-century English one, decorated with four cherubs.

4. The longest-lived wine is probably Madeira, and bottles from the eighteenth century are drinkable.

5. Vines grown in sand are free from bugs and many diseases. Examples are Colares from Portugal and wine from the Listel company in the south of France.

6. The most dangerous vineyard in the world is Château Musar in the Bekaa Valley in Lebanon. In one year, the fighting made it impossible to make wine.

7. The smallest Appellation Contrôlée by production in France is Château Grillet, a single property of six acres in the Rhône, producing hugely expensive 300–400 cases of wine a year. By area, the smallest AC is La Romanée in Burgundy.

8. The third largest producer of wine in the world is Russia. Will they soon follow the Bulgarians by selling us cheap wine?

9. Possibly the oldest wine-making concern in Italy is the Ricasoli family site in Tuscany, dating from 1141, now owned by Seagram.

10. Probably the oldest winery in Australia in continuous production is Olive Farm, founded in 1829.

11. The most unlikely wine-making concern in the world is that which makes the sparkling wine called Omar Khayyam, outside Bombay in India.

12. The earliest-picked grapes are picked in Germany at 4 am on the first winter morning to reach −7°C, to make Eiswein.

13. The first famous vintage we know of was a Roman one of 121 BC, which was still being drunk 200 years later.

14. Clos de Vougeot in Burgundy is probably the most intensively owned property in the world; its 124 acres are owned by over eighty different people.

15. Different crop yields can range from 15 hectolitres of wine per hectare of vineyard at Château Rayas in Châteauneuf-du-Pape, to over 80 hectolitres in parts of Germany.

16. Some wine-makers pasteurize their wine. Most who do won't admit it, but one of the few who does is Louis Latour in Burgundy.

17. In California wine-producers who sometimes have to transport their grapes great distances by truck do so at night, to prevent the grapes fermenting in the heat of the sun.

18. The most patriotic wine-drinking country in Europe is Portugal, where they mostly drink their own wine. Apart from Albania, of course, where they have no choice.

19. Champagne was not the first wine with bubbles in it; that giant leap for mankind is claimed by Blanquette de Limoux in south-west France.

20. The most planted grape variety in the world is the Airen, which covers huge areas of Spain. The general view is that it also produces more boring wine than any other.

And one more: the Duke of Clarence drowned in a butt of Malmsey Madeira. The only way to go.

Appendix 2

Auctioneers

Bigwood Auctioneers
The Old School, Tiddington, Stratford-upon-Avon, Warwickshire,
CV37 7AW (Tel: 0789-69415)
4 per year.

Christie's
8 King St, London, SW1Y 6QT (Tel: 071-839 9060)
85 Old Brompton Rd, London, SW7 3LD (Tel: 071-581 7611)
56–60 Gresham St, London, EC2V 7BB (Tel: 071-588 4424)
164–166 Bath St, Glasgow, G2 4TB (Tel: 041-332 8134)
Up to 50 per year.

International Wine Auctions
40 Victoria Way, London, SE7 7QS (Tel: 081-293 4992)
6 per year.

Lacy Scott
10 Risbygate St, Bury St Edmunds, Suffolk, IP33 3AA (Tel: 0284-763531)
1 per year, just before Christmas.

Lithgow Sons & Partners
The Auction House, Station Rd, Stokesley, Middlesbrough, Cleveland (Tel: 0642-710158)
2 per year, December and June.

Phillips, Son, & Neil
39 Park End St, Oxford, OX1 1JD (Tel: 0865-723524)
5 per year.

Sotheby's
34–35 New Bond St, London, W1A 2AA (Tel: 071-493 8080)
Summers Place, Billingshurst, West Sussex, RH14 9AD (Tel: 040 381-3933)
10–12 per year.

Wine Merchants

Anthony Byrne Fine Wines
88 High St, Ramsey, Huntingdon, Cambs, PE17 1BS (Tel: 0487-814555)

Avery's
7 Park St, Bristol, BS1 5NG (Tel: 0272-214141)

Nigel Baring
20d Ranston St, London, NW1 6SY (Tel: 071-724 0836)

Berry Bros & Rudd
3 St James's, London, SW1A 1EG (Tel: 071-839 9033)
The Wine Shop, Hamilton Close, Houndmills, Basingstoke, Hants, RG21 2YH (Tel: 0256-23566)

Bibendum
113 Regent's Park Rd, London, NW1 8UR (Tel: 071: 586 9761)

Bottoms Up
Astra House, Edinburgh Way, Harlow, Essex, CM20 2BE (Tel: 0279-453408)

Buckingham Trading Co.
68 Alpha St, Slough, Bucks, SL1 1Q7 (Tel: 0753-21336)

Christopher Piper Wines
1 Silver St, Ottery St Mary, Devon, EX11 1DB (Tel: 040481-4139/2197)

College Cellar/La Réserve
56 Walton St, London, SW3 1RB (Tel: 071-589 2020)

Corney & Barrow
12 Helmet Row, London, EC1V 3QJ (Tel: 071-251 4051)

Domaine Direct
29 Wilmington Sq, London WC1X 0EG (Tel: 071-837 3521/1142)

Michael Druit Wines
9 Deanery St, London, W1Y 5LF (Tel: 071-493 5412)

Eldridge Pope
Weymouth Ave, Dorchester, Dorset, DT1 1QT (Tel: 0305-251251)
(Ten branches, one called Godrich & Petman, two called Reynier Wine Libraries)

Farr Vintners
19 Sussex St, London, SW1V 4RR (Tel: 071-828 1960)

R. C. Gold
Park House, Church Rd, Saffron Walden, Essex (Tel: 0799-40699)

Ernst Gorge
245 Whitechapel Rd, London, E1 1DB (Tel: 071-247 1324)

Great American Wine Company (wholesalers)
J. O. Sims Building, Winchester Walk, London, SE1 9DG (Tel: 071-407 0502)

Hayes, Hanson & Clark
17 Lettice St, London, SW6 4EH (Tel: 071-736 7878)

Hungerford Wine Co.
Unit 3, Station Yard, Hungerford, Berks, RG17 0DY (Tel: 0488-683238)

Richard Kihl
164 Regent's Park Rd, London, NW3 8XN (Tel: 071-586 5911)

Kurtz and Chan Wines
1 Duke of York St, London, SW1 6JP (Tel: 071-930 6981)

Les Amis du Vin
19 Charlotte St, London, W1P 1HP (Tel: 071-636 4020)

Majestic Wine Warehouses
421 New King's Rd, London, SW6 4RN (Tel: 071-736 1515)
(30 branches nationwide)

Marks & Spencer
57 Baker St, London, W1A 1DN (Tel: 071-935 4422)
(263 branches nationwide)

Mistral Wines
5 Junction Mews, Sale Place, London W2 1PN (Tel: 071-262 5437)

Moreno Wines
11 Marylands Rd, London, W9 2DU (Tel: 071-286 0678)
2 Norfolk Place, London, W2 1QN (071-723 6897)

Morris & Verdin
28 Churton St, London, SW1V 2LP (Tel: 071-630 8888)

Oddbins
31–33 Weir Rd, Durnsford Industrial Estate, London, SW19 8UG
(Tel: 081-879 1199)
(142 branches nationwide)

Thos Peating
Westgate House, Bury St Edmunds, Suffolk, IP33 1QS (Tel: 0284-755948)
(32 branches in the east)

Peter Dominic
Astra House, Edinburgh Way, Harlow, Essex, CM20 2BE (Tel: 0279-453408)
(800 branches nationwide)

Safeway
6 Millington Rd, Hayes, Middlesex UB3 4AY (Tel: 081-848 8744)
(250 branches nationwide)

J. Sainsbury
Stamford House, Stamford St, London, SE1 9LL (Tel: 071-921 6000)
(280 stores nationwide)

Tanners Wines
26 Wyle Cop, Shrewsbury, Shropshire, SY1 1XD (Tel: 0743-232400)
(6 branches in the north-west)

Tesco
New Tesco House, PO Box 18, Delamare Rd, Cheshunt, Herts
EN8 9SL (Tel: 0992-32222)
(350 stores nationwide)

The Wine Society
Gunnels Wood Rd, Stevenage, Herts, SG1 2BG (Tel: 0438-741177)

Thresher
Sefton House, 42 Church St, Welwyn Garden City, Herts, AL8 6PJ
(Tel: 0707-328244)
(960 branches nationwide)

Unwins
Birchwood House, Victoria St, Dartford, Kent, DA1 5AJ (Tel: 0322-72711)
(300 branches)

Victor Hugo Wines
Bath Street Wine Cellar, 15 Bath St, St Helier, Jersey, Channel Islands
(Tel: 0534-20237)
(other branches in the Channel Islands)

Victoria Wine
Brook House, Chertsey Rd, Woking, Surrey, GU21 5BE (Tel: 0483-715066)
(850 branches nationwide)

Waitrose
171 Victoria St, London, SW1E 5NN (Tel: 071-838 1000)
(85 stores)

Winecellars
153/5 Wandsworth High St, London SW18 4JB (Tel: 081-871 2668)

Yapp Brothers
The Old Brewery, Water St, Mere, Wilts, BA12 6DY (Tel: 0747-860423)

Youngs & Co.
21 Barnaby St, London, SW10 0PR (Tel: 071-351 1990)

Appendix 3

The wines of the world – how long to keep them

Below is a list of generally available wines and how long they usually need from their vintage date to reach maturity. It goes without saying that this is only a rough guide and that better, and usually more expensive, examples of each wine will last longer. Vintage differences will also affect the pace of maturity. In the following list, 'asap' means exactly that, 'n' means now – it can be drunk from the vintage.

If you prefer to drink younger wines then lean towards the earlier end of an age range, and vice versa. Some of these age ranges are perhaps controversially long or short, but most are the result of experience, received wisdom, discussion, or from an industry consensus including Hugh Johnson, Jancis Robinson and others.

Aged Tawny Port, now
Aligoté, n–2
Almacenista Sherry, n–3
Aloxe-Corton, 4–15
Alto Adige, w, 1–3
Alto Adige, r, asap
Amarone, 5–17
Amontillado Sherry, now
Anjou, w, asap
Anjou, r, asap
Anjou, s, 5–20
Auslese, 5–20+
Badan, asap
Bairrada, w, 1–4
Bairrada, r, 2–6
Bandol, 2–10+
Banyuls, 4–20+
Barbaresco, 5–17
Barbera, n–4
Bardolino, asap
Barolo, 5–20+
Barsac, 3–20+
Beaune, 3–7
Beaujolais, asap
Beaujolais Villages, 2–10

Bergerac, w, asap
Bergerac, r, 1–5+
Blaye, 2–5
Bonnezeaux, 4–20+
Bordeaux, w, asap
Bordeaux, r, 1–3
Bordeaux, s, n–2
Botrytis, 4–?
Bourg, 1–4
Bourgogne, w, 1–3
Bourgogne, r, 1–5
Bourgogne, Hautes-Côtes, 1–4
Bourgogne Passe-tout-grains, 2–6
Bourgueil, 1–4
Brouilly, 2–5
Brunello di Montalcino, 7–20+
Buzet, 3–7
Cadillac, 2–5+
Cahors, 2–10+
Carmignano, 3–8
Cérons, 2–5
Chablis, 3–5
Chablis, Grand Cru, 5–12
Chablis, Premier Cru, 3–6

Chambolle-Musigny, 5–15
Chardonnay, 1–7
Chassagne-Montrachet, 2–10
Châteauneuf-du-Pape, w, asap–3
Châteauneuf-du-Pape, r, 3–10
Chénas, 2–5
Chenin Blanc, n–4
Chianti, 2–5
Chianti Classico, 4–10
Chinon, n–4
Chiroubles, 2–5
Chorey-les-Beaune, 2–8
Colares, 10–30+
Commandaria, n–4
Condrieu, 2–4
Coonawarra, 4–20+
Corbières, w, asap
Corbières, r, 2–10
Cornas, 5–20+
Corse, w, asap
Corse, r, 3–8
Corton-Charlemagne, 5–20
Coteaux du Layon, 2–20
Coteaux du Tricastin, asap
Côte Rôtie, 8–20+
Côtes de Brouilly, 2–5
Côtes de Duras, 2–4
Côtes du Frontonnais, asap
Côtes du Luberon, w, asap
Côtes du Luberon, r, n–5
Côtes du Rhône, w, n–1
Côtes du Rhône, r, 2–6
Côtes du Roussillon, 2–4
Côtes du Ventoux, asap
Crozes-Hermitage, w, 1–4
Crozes-Hermitage, r, 3–6
Cru Bourgeois, 4–15
Cru Classé, 6–30+
Crusted Port, 2–8

Dão, w, asap
Dão, r, 1–10
Dolcetto, asap
Edelzwicker, asap
Eiswein, 2–8+
Entre-Deux-Mers, asap
Faugères, 1–5
Fitou, 1–6
Fixin, 2–6
Fleurie, 2–5
Franken, 2–5
Frascati, asap–2
Fronsac, 5–15
Gaillac, n–4
Galestro, asap
Galicia, asap
Gavi, 1–4
Gevrey-Chambertin, 5–15
Gewürztraminer, 2–5
Gigondas, 3–10
Givry, 2–5
Goldenmuskateller, 2–5
Grand Cru, 5–25
Graves, w, 3–30
Graves, r, 3–10
Gros Plant, n–4
Grüner Veltliner, 1–5+
Gumpoldskirchen, 2–5
Haut-Poitou, 1–3
Hermitage, w, n–7
Hermitage, r, 5–30+
Juliénas, 2–8
Jumilia, 1–4
Jura, w, 1–4
Jura, s, 5–30
Jurançon, 2–10+
Kabinett, 2–10
La Mancha, w/r, asap
Lambrusco, w/r, asap
Landwein, asap
Languedoc, w, n–5

Languedoc, r, 1–5
Late Bottled Vintage Port, now
Late Harvest, 5–20+
Liebfraumilch, asap
Liqueur Muscat, n–+
Lirac, 1–4
Listrac, 2–7
Listel, asap
Loupiac, 2–8
Lugana, n–3
Mâcon, w, 2–5
Mâcon, r, n–2
Madeira, n–+
Madiran, 4–12
Margaret River, w, 2–8
Margaret River, r, 4–15
Margaux, 4–10+
Mas de Daumas Gassac,
   10–20+
Mercurey, w, 3–5
Mercurey, r, 2–5
Meursault, 2–6
Meursault, Premier Cru,
   4–15
Minervois, n–10
Monbazillac, 2–10+
Montagny, 2–6
Montepulciano d'Abruzzo,
   2–6
Monthélie, 2–8
Montlouis, w, 2–10+
Montlouis, s, 5–20
Montrachet, 6–20
Morey Saint-Denis, 4–15+
Morgon, 3–8
Moscatel de Sétubal, n–+
Moscato, asap
Moulin-à-Vent, 3–10+
Moulis, 2–6+
Muscadet, n–5+
Muscat d'Alsace, n–3

Navarra, n–5
Nouveau, asap
Novello, asap
Nuits-St-Georges, 5–15
Orvieto, asap–3
Orvieto, Abboccato, 2–4
Pacherenc du Vic-Bilh, 2–8
Pauillac, 5–10
Penedès, w, asap–4
Penedès, r, 2–10+
Pernand-Vergelesses, w, 2–5
Pernand-Vergelesses, r, 2–7
Picolit, 3–6
Pinot Blanc, n–3
Pinot Grigio, asap
Pomerol, 4–20+
Pommard, 3–15
Pouilly-Fuissé/Vinzelles, 2–6
Pouilly Fumé, n–5+
Premières Côtes de Bordeaux,
   2–7
Prosecco, asap
Provence, w, n–2
Provence, r, n–4
Pugligny-Montrachet, 2–5
Pugligny-Montrachet,
   Premier Cru, 4–10
QbA, asap
QmP, 2–20+
Quarts de Chaume, 5–20+
Quinta Port, 7–20+
Raboso, 4–8
Rasteau, r, 2–4
Rasteau, s, asap
Recioto, 4–10+
Regnié, 1–3
Retsina, asap
Ribera del Duero, 5–15+
Rioja, w, asap–10+
Rioja, r, n–20+
Rivesaltes, now

Roussillon, w, n–3
Roussillon, r, 1–5
Ruby Port, asap
Rully, w, 2–5
Rully, r, 3–6
St Amour, 2–5
St-Aubin, 2–5
St Chinian, 2–6
Ste-Croix-du-Mont, 2–10
St Emilion, 2–20+
St Estèphe, 4–15
St-Joseph, 2–8
St Julien, 5–10
St Péray, asap
St Purçain, asap
St Romain, 2–5
St Véran, 1–4
Sancerre, w, n–10
Sancerre, r, asap
Sangiovese di Romagna,
    asap
Santenay, 3–5
Saumur, w, asap
Saumur, s, 4–10+
Sauternes, 2–+
Savennières, 4–20
Savoie, 2–6
Schluck, asap
Sélection de Graines
    Nobles, 8–40+
Soave, asap–5
Spätlese, 2–10+
Sylvaner, 1–4
Tafelwein, asap
Taurasi, 6–15
Tawney Port, now

Tokai, asap
Tokay Aszu, 5–20+
Tokay Szamorodni, now
Tokay d'Alsace, 2–4
Torcolato, 4–8
Torgiano, 5–15
Toro, 3–8
Trebbiano, asap–4
Trockenbeerenauslese,
    5–60+
Vacqueyras, 2–6
Valdepeñas, 2–6
Valpolicella, asap–5
VDQS, 1–5
Vendange Tardive, 5–20+
Verdicchio, asap–2
Verduzzo, w, asap
Verduzzo, r, 2–10
Villages, n–4
Vin de Pays, asap–2
Vin de Table, asap
Vinho Maduro, n–+
Vinho Verde, asap
Vino da Tavola, asap/5–15
Vino Nobile di Montepulciano,
    4–10+
Vin Santo, now
Vintage Character Port, now
Vintage Port, 15–40
Volnay, 4–12
Vosne-Romanée, 5–15
Vougeot, 5–17
Vouvray, w, 2–20
Vouvray, r, 5–30
Weissburgunder (Pinot Blanc),
    n–3+

The ageing potential of the principle grape varieties

Cabernet Sauvignon, 4–50+
Cabernet Franc, 2–20+
Chardonnay, 2–10/15
Chenin Blanc, 2–20+
Columbard, 1–4
Gewürztraminer, 2–20+
Kerner, 2–6
Marsanne, 2–6
Mavrud, 3–10
Melnik, 4–10

Merlot, 3–30+
Müller-Thurgau, n–5
Nebbiolo, 3–15+
Pinot Noir, 2–20
Riesling, 3–40+
Sauvignon Blanc, 3–20
Sémillon, 2–15
Syrah, 3–30
Zinfandel, 3–10+

Bibliography

Below are some books that are useful pointers in other directions.

Andrew Barr, *Wine Snobbery*, Faber & Faber, 1988
Nick Belfrage, *Life Beyond Lambrusco*, Sidgwick & Jackson, 1985
Michael Busselle, *The Wine Lovers' Guide to France*, Michael Joseph, 1987
David Gleave, *The Wines of Italy*, Salamander Books, 1989
Anthony Hanson, *Burgundy*, Faber & Faber, 1982 (new edition soon)
Hugh Johnson, *The World Atlas of Wine*, Mitchell Beazley, 1985
— *The Wine Companion*, Mitchell Beazley, 1987 (new edition soon)
— *Pocket Wine Book*, Mitchell Beazley, annual
— *The Story of Wine*, Mitchell Beazley, 1989
Simon Loftus, *Anatomy of the Wine Trade*, Sidgwick & Jackson, 1985
Jane MacQuitty, *Champagne and Sparkling Wines*, Mitchell Beazley, 1986
Charles Metcalfe and Kathryn McWhirter, *The Wines of Spain and Portugal*, Salamander Books, 1988
Robert Parker, *Bordeaux – The Definitive Guide*, Dorling Kindersley, 1986
— *The Wines of the Rhone Valley and Provence*, Dorling Kindersley, 1988
— *The Wine Buyer's Guide*, Dorling Kindersley, 1989
Edmund Penning-Rowsell, *The Wines of Bordeaux*, Penguin, 1985
Jancis Robinson, *Vintage Timecharts*, Mitchell Beazley, 1989
— *Vines, Grapes, and Wines*, Mitchell Beazley, 1986 (revised edition 1987)

Index

References to countries and regions are usually of a general nature, with particular wines from countries and regions being indicated by the subheading 'examples'. In the case of the principal wine-producing countries (France, Germany, Italy and Spain) and the largest regions of France (Bordeaux, Burgundy and the south), only general references have been indexed.